Kaplan Publishing are constantly fin
ways to make a difference to your st
exciting online resources really do c
different to students looking for exc...

C000319477

This book comes with free MyKaplan online resources so that you can study anytime, anywhere. This free online resource is not sold separately and is included in the price of the book.

Having purchased this book, you have access to the following online study materials:

CONTENT	ACCA (including FFA,FAB,FMA)		FIA (excluding FFA,FAB,FMA)	
	Text	Kit	Text	Kit
Eletronic version of the book	✓	✓	✓	✓
Check Your Understanding Test with instant answers	✓			
Material updates	✓	✓	✓	✓
Latest official ACCA exam questions*		✓		
Extra question assistance using the signpost icon**		✓		
Timed questions with an online tutor debrief using clock icon***		✓		
Interim assessment including questions and answers	✓		✓	
Technical answers	✓	✓	✓	✓

*   Excludes F1, F2, F3, F4, FAB, FMA and FFA; for all other papers includes a selection of questions, as released by ACCA

**   For ACCA P1–P7 only

*** Excludes F1, F2, F3, F4, FAB, FMA and FFA

How to access your online resources

Kaplan Financial students will already have a MyKaplan account and these extra resources will be available to you online. You do not need to register again, as this process was completed when you enrolled. If you are having problems accessing online materials, please ask your course administrator.

If you are not studying with Kaplan and did not purchase your book via a Kaplan website, to unlock your extra online resources please go to www.mykaplan.co.uk/addabook (even if you have set up an account and registered books previously). You will then need to enter the ISBN number (on the title page and back cover) and the unique pass key number contained in the scratch panel below to gain access.

You will also be required to enter additional information during this process to set up or confirm your account details.

If you purchased through Kaplan Flexible Learning or via the Kaplan Publishing website you will automatically receive an e-mail invitation to MyKaplan. Please register your details using this email to gain access to your content. If you do not receive the e-mail or book content, please contact Kaplan Publishing.

Your Code and Information

This code can only be used once for the registration of one book online. This registration and your online content will expire when the final sittings for the examinations covered by this book have taken place. Please allow one hour from the time you submit your book details for us to process your request.

Please scratch the film to access your MyKaplan code.

z3N1-8V6H-s6pB-MlxJ

Please be aware that this code is case-sensitive and you will need to include the dashes within the passcode, but not when entering the ISBN. For further technical support, please visit www.MyKaplan.co.uk

Paper F4 (ENG)

Corporate and Business Law

EXAM KIT

British Library Cataloguing-in-Publication Data

A catalogue record for this book is available from the British Library.

Published by:

Kaplan Publishing UK

Unit 2 The Business Centre

Molly Millar's Lane

Wokingham

Berkshire

RG41 2QZ

ISBN: 978-1-78415-827-9

Acknowledgements

The past ACCA examination questions are the copyright of the Association of Chartered Certified Accountants. The original answers to the questions from June 1994 onwards were produced by the examiners themselves and have been adapted by Kaplan Publishing.

We are grateful to the Chartered Institute of Management Accountants and the Institute of Chartered Accountants in England and Wales for permission to reproduce past examination questions. The answers have been prepared by Kaplan Publishing.

CONTENTS

Section

New features in this edition

In addition to providing a wide ranging bank of practice questions, we have also included in this edition:

- Examples of new-style 'multi-task' questions that will form part of the new examination format.
- Paper specific information and advice on exam technique.
- Our recommended approach to make your revision for this particular subject as effective as possible.

You will find a wealth of other resources to help you with your studies on the following sites:

www.mykaplan.co.uk and www.**acca**global.com/students/

Quality and accuracy are of the utmost importance to us so if you spot an error in any of our products, please send an email to mykaplanreporting@kaplan.com with full details.

Our Quality Co-ordinator will work with our technical team to verify the error and take action to ensure it is corrected in future editions.

INDEX TO QUESTIONS AND ANSWERS

INTRODUCTION

The style of the Paper F4 exam changed from September 2014.

Accordingly, the old ACCA scenario questions have been adapted to reflect the new style of paper.

These questions have been labelled with an (A) next to them.

The format of questions for multi-task questions differs between the paper based exam and the computer based exam. Each multi-task question has been labelled either CBE (computer based exam) or PBE (paper based exam) as appropriate.

MULTIPLE CHOICE QUESTIONS

MULTI-TASK QUESTIONS

EXAM TECHNIQUE

- **Do not skip any of the material** in the syllabus.

- **Read each question** *very* carefully.

- **Double-check your answer** before committing yourself to it.

- Answer **every** question – if you do not know an answer, you don't lose anything by guessing. Think carefully before you **guess**. The examiner has indicated that many candidates are still leaving blank answers in the real exam.

- If you are answering a multiple-choice question, **eliminate first those answers that you know are wrong**. Then choose the most appropriate answer from those that are left.

- **Don't panic** if you realise you've answered a question incorrectly. Getting one question wrong will not mean the difference between passing and failing

Computer-based exams – tips

- Do not attempt a CBE until you have **completed all study material** relating to it.

- On the ACCA website there is a CBE demonstration. It is **ESSENTIAL** that you attempt this before your real CBE. You will become familiar with how to move around the CBE screens and the way that questions are formatted, increasing your confidence and speed in the actual exam.

- Be sure you understand how to use the **software** before you start the exam. If in doubt, ask the assessment centre staff to explain it to you.

- Questions are **displayed on the screen** and answers are entered using keyboard and mouse. At the end of the exam, you are given a certificate showing the result you have achieved.

PAPER SPECIFIC INFORMATION

THE EXAM

FORMAT OF THE PAPER-BASED AND COMPUTER-BASED EXAM

	Number of marks
45 compulsory multiple-choice questions (1 or 2 marks each)	70
5 multi-task questions (6 marks each)	30

Total time allowed: 2 hours

- The examinations contain 100% compulsory questions and students must study across the breadth of the syllabus to prepare effectively for the examination

- The examination will be assessed by a two hour paper-based or computer-based examination

PASS MARK

The pass mark for all ACCA Qualification examination papers is 50%.

DETAILED SYLLABUS

The detailed syllabus and study guide written by the ACCA can be found at:

www.accaglobal.com/students/

KAPLAN'S RECOMMENDED REVISION APPROACH

QUESTION PRACTICE IS THE KEY TO SUCCESS

Success in professional examinations relies upon you acquiring a firm grasp of the required knowledge at the tuition phase. In order to be able to do the questions, knowledge is essential.

However, the difference between success and failure often hinges on your exam technique on the day and making the most of the revision phase of your studies.

The **Kaplan Study Text** is the starting point, designed to provide the underpinning knowledge to tackle all questions. However, in the revision phase, pouring over text books is not the answer.

Kaplan online progress tests help you consolidate your knowledge and understanding and are a useful tool to check whether you can remember key topic areas.

Kaplan Pocket Notes are designed to help you quickly revise a topic area, however you then need to practice questions. There is a need to progress to full exam standard questions as soon as possible, and to tie your exam technique and technical knowledge together.

The importance of question practice cannot be over-emphasised.

The recommended approach below is designed by expert tutors in the field, in conjunction with their knowledge of the examiner.

The approach taken for the fundamental papers is to revise by topic area.

You need to practice as many questions as possible in the time you have left.

OUR AIM

Our aim is to get you to the stage where you can attempt exam standard questions confidently, to time, in a closed book environment, with no supplementary help (i.e. to simulate the real examination experience).

Practising your exam technique on real past examination questions, in timed conditions, is also vitally important for you to assess your progress and identify areas of weakness that may need more attention in the final run up to the examination.

The approach below shows you which questions you should use to build up to coping with exam standard question practice, and references to the sources of information available should you need to revisit a topic area in more detail.

Remember that in the real examination, all you have to do is:

- attempt all questions required by the exam

- only spend the allotted time on each question, and

- get them at least 50% right!

Try and practice this approach on every question you attempt from now to the real exam.

THE KAPLAN PAPER F4 REVISION PLAN

Stage 1: Assess areas of strengths and weaknesses

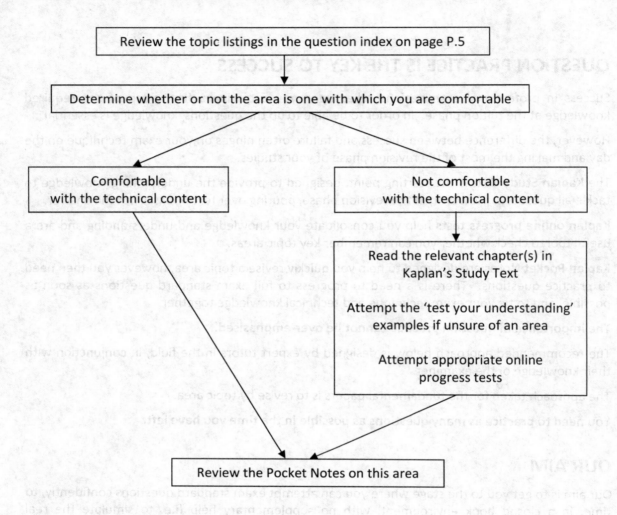

Review the topic listings in the question index on page P.5

Determine whether or not the area is one with which you are comfortable

Comfortable with the technical content

Not comfortable with the technical content

Read the relevant chapter(s) in Kaplan's Study Text

Attempt the 'test your understanding' examples if unsure of an area

Attempt appropriate online progress tests

Review the Pocket Notes on this area

Stage 2: Practice questions

Ensure that you revise all syllabus areas as questions could be asked on anything.

Try to avoid referring to text books and notes and the model answer until you have completed your attempt.

Try to answer the question in the allotted time.

Review your attempt with the model answer. If you got the answer wrong, can you see why? Was the problem a lack of knowledge or a failure to understand the question fully?

Fill in the self-assessment box below and decide on your best course of action.

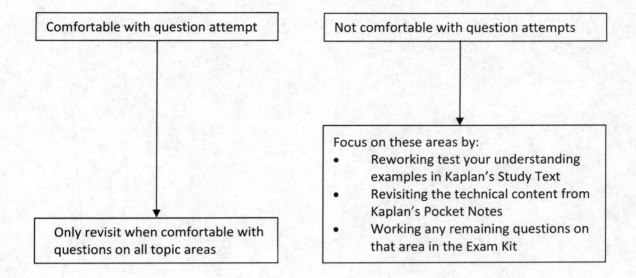

Stage 3: Final pre-exam revision

We recommend that you **attempt at least one two hour mock examination** containing a set of previously unseen exam standard questions.

It is important that you get a feel for the breadth of coverage of a real exam without advanced knowledge of the topic areas covered – just as you will expect to see on the real exam day.

Ideally this mock should be sat in timed, closed book, real exam conditions and could be:

- a mock examination offered by your tuition provider, and/or

- the pilot paper in the back of this Exam Kit

Section 1

MULTIPLE CHOICE QUESTIONS

ESSENTIAL ELEMENTS OF THE LEGAL SYSTEM

1   Which of the following statements regarding 'common law' is NOT correct?

    A   It is the body of law as made by judges through the determination of cases

    B   It is law created by Parliament

    C   It is the system of law that emerged following the Norman Conquest in 1066

                                        (1 mark)

2   Which of the following is NOT a track to which a civil case can be allocated?

    A   The small claims track

    B   The fast track

    C   The high value track   **(1 mark)**

3   In relation to the English Legal System, where did the common law originate from?

    A   Acts of Parliament

    B   Delegated legislation

    C   Custom   **(1 mark)**

4   Which of the following would NOT be regarded as persuasive precedent by a judge within the Court of Appeal?

    A   Decisions of lower courts

    B   Decisions of the Supreme Court

    C   Obiter dicta statements   **(1 mark)**

5   Which of the following is the name used for the person who commences a civil action?

    A   Appellant

    B   Plaintiff

    C   Claimant   **(1 mark)**

6 Which part of a legal judgement establishes the precedent that is to be followed by lower courts?

A   The ratio decidendi

B   The facts that are considered important by the judge

C   The obiter dicta   **(1 mark)**

7 Which is the final appeal court in the United Kingdom?

A   The High Court

B   The Supreme Court

C   The Court of Appeal   **(1 mark)**

8 Which of the following is NOT a form of delegated legislation?

A   Statute

B   Statutory instruments

C   Orders in Council   **(1 mark)**

9 Which of the following statements regarding the Supreme Court is correct?

A   It is bound by its previous decisions, but it may depart if they are considered to be wrong.

B   It is always bound by its previous decisions.

C   It is normally bound by its previous decisions, but may depart when it appears right to do so.   **(1 mark)**

10 Which of the following is NOT one of the stages for creating an Act of Parliament?

A   Third reading

B   Fourth reading

C   Committee stage   **(1 mark)**

11 What is the standard of proof required in a criminal case?

A   On the balance of probabilities

B   The defence establishes a reasonable defence to the allegations

C   Beyond any doubt

D   Beyond reasonable doubt   **(2 marks)**

12   **Which of the following statements regarding judicial precedent is correct?**

A   The Court of Appeal is bound by judgements of the Supreme Court.

B   The Court of Appeal is bound by judgements of the Queen's Bench Division of the High Court.

C   The Court of Appeal is bound by judgements of the Chancery Division of the High Court.

D   The Court of Appeal is bound by judgements of the Family Division of the High Court.

(2 marks)

13   **Which of the following is NOT a division of the High Court?**

A   The Chancery Division

B   The Family Division

C   The Queen's Bench Division

D   The Supreme Division   **(2 marks)**

14   **What does the term 'private law' refer to?**

A   The body of laws that derive from the deciding of cases

B   The body of laws that seek to regulate the relationship between individuals

C   The legal principle that states that a person has the right to privacy

D   The body of laws that seeks to regulate the relationship between the State and its citizens   **(2 marks)**

15   **In the context of case law which of the following statements is correct?**

A   Distinguishing occurs when a higher court changes the decision reached by a lower court.

B   Distinguishing occurs when a court changes the law stated in a previous case.

C   Distinguishing occurs when a court indicates that the facts of a previous case are different.

D   Distinguishing occurs when a court indicated that the material facts of a previous case are different.   **(2 marks)**

16   **The decisions of magistrates' courts in criminal cases can be appealed to which TWO of the following courts?**

(i)   The Crown Court

(ii)   The High Court

(iii) The Court of Appeal

(iv)   The Supreme Court

A   (i) and (ii)

B   (i) and (iii)

C   (ii) and (iii)

D   (iii) and (iv)   **(2 marks)**

17 Which of the following is regarded as private law?

    (i)   Criminal law

    (ii)   Contract law

    A   (i) only

    B   (ii) only

    C   Both (i) and (ii)

    D   Neither (i) or (ii)   **(2 marks)**

18 Which of the following statement/s regarding common law and equity is/are correct?

    (i)   If the common law and equity conflict, then the common law prevails

    (ii)   Equity was developed to introduce fairness

    A   (i) only

    B   (ii) only

    C   Both (i) and (ii)

    D   Neither (i) or (ii)   **(2 marks)**

19 Which of the following statement/s regarding civil law is/are correct?

    (i)   It is the body of laws that does NOT relate to criminal offences

    (ii)   It is law created by judges through decision made in cases

    A   (i) only

    B   (ii) only

    C   Both (i) and (ii)

    D   Neither (i) or (ii)   **(2 marks)**

20 What is the name of the process by which the courts can challenge delegated legislation?

    A   Judges renewal

    B   Judicial renewal

    C   Judges review

    D   Judicial review   **(2 marks)**

21 When does a Parliamentary Bill become an Act of Parliament?

    A   When it passes through the committee stage

    B   On receiving its third reading

    C   When passed by both Houses of Parliament

    D   On receiving the Royal Assent   **(2 marks)**

22 **What does the 'literal rule' of statutory interpretation mean?**

A   Words should be given their ordinary meaning.

B   Word meanings can be gathered from their context.

C   Words should be given the meaning which is likely to give effect to the purpose or reform which the statute intended.

D   Words should be given their ordinary grammatical meaning unless the meaning is manifestly absurd.
(2 marks)

23 **Which of the following courts deal with civil law matters only?**

A   The Crown Court

B   The magistrates' court

C   The county court
(1 mark)

24 **Which of the following is an English court NORMALLY bound to follow?**

A   An obiter statement of a higher court

B   A ratio of a lower court

C   A ratio of a court at the same level

D   An obiter statement of the Supreme Court
(2 marks)

25 **Which of the following courts hear appeals from the Magistrates' court?**

(1)   County court

(2)   Crown court

(3)   High Court

A   (1) and (2)

B   (2) and (3)

C   (1) and (3)

D   (1), (2) and (3)
(2 marks)

26 **Which TWO of the following are private law actions?**

(1)   Those between individuals

(2)   Those between business organisations

(3)   Those between individuals and the state

A   (1) and (2)

B   (1) and (3)

C   (2) and (3)
(1 mark)

27   Which of the following court is NOT a source of English law?

      A   Custom

      B   Equity

      C   Public law   (1 mark)

28   Which of the following is an example of the purposive approach to statutory
      interpretation?

      A   The mischief rule

      B   The literal rule

      C   The golden rule   (1 mark)

29   Which of the following correctly applies to the burden of proof in a criminal case?

      A   It must be proved beyond reasonable doubt

      B   It must be proved on the balance of probabilities

      C   It lies with the prosecution

      D   It lies with the defence   (2 marks)

THE LAW OF OBLIGATIONS

30   In the context of contract law, what will a display of goods in a shop window generally
      constitute?

      A   An offer

      B   An invitation to treat

      C   A statement of intention   (1 mark)

31   When is acceptance not effective?

      A   If through conduct only

      B   If through express words only

      C   Through the offeree's non-communicated intention   (1 mark)

32   Where the post is a valid means of acceptance, at what point will the offeree have been
      held to have accepted the offer?

      A   When the letter of acceptance has been written

      B   When the letter of acceptance has been correctly addressed, its postage paid, and
             posted

      C   When the letter of acceptance is received by the offeror   (1 mark)

33 **Which of the following correctly describes a warranty?**

A A lesser term in a contract

B The most important term in a contract

C Not a term of a contract at all **(1 mark)**

34 **What will be the effect where the nature of an exclusion clause is misrepresented by the person wishing to rely on it?**

A It will fail to protect the party attempting to rely on it

B The misrepresentation will reduce any award by the court by 50%

C It will have no impact where the party has signed a document containing the clause **(1 mark)**

35 **Which of the following is NOT a type of term?**

A Warranty

B Condition

C Representation **(1 mark)**

36 **Which of the following is NOT included in an assessment of damages in contract law?**

A Remoteness of damage

B Mitigation

C The sum identified in a penalty clause **(1 mark)**

37 **Which of the following is NOT an equitable remedy?**

A Damages

B Specific performance

C Injunction **(1 mark)**

38 **Breach of which term would NOT entitle the innocent party to repudiate the contract?**

A A warranty

B A condition

C An innominate term **(1 mark)**

39 **What are the requirements for a valid and binding contract?**

A Offer and acceptance only

B Offer, acceptance and consideration only

C Offer, acceptance, consideration and intention to create legal relations **(1 mark)**

40   Which of the following statements about executory consideration is correct?

A   It is consideration that is yet to be provided

B   It is consideration that has already been provided

C   It is consideration that is insufficient in the eyes of the law

(1 mark)

41   Which of the following is NOT an essential element of a valid simple contract?

A   The contract must be in writing

B   The parties must be in agreement

C   Each party must provide consideration

(1 mark)

42   What does an agreement to carry out an act which the law requires anyway amount to?

A   Sufficient consideration

B   Insufficient consideration

C   Past consideration

(1 mark)

43   What is an exclusion clause?

A   It is a clause excluding the rights of persons other than the contracting parties to sue for breach of contract

B   It is a clause which limits the contractual capacity of one of the parties

C   It is a contractual clause which limits liability for breach of contract

(1 mark)

44   What is it called when one party announces their intention NOT to honour his agreement before the performance was due?

A   Anticipatory breach

B   Actual breach

C   Fundamental breach

(1 mark)

45   Where there has been an anticipatory breach of contract when is the injured party NOT entitled to sue?

A   After a reasonable time

B   From the moment the other party indicates that he does not intend to be bound

C   From the moment the other party actually breaches a contractual condition

(1 mark)

46   Which of the following types of contract must be in writing?

A   A partnership agreement

B   A contract for the sale of goods

C   An agreement for the transfer of land

(1 mark)

47   Which of the following is NOT required for revocation of an offer to be effective?

A   It must be in writing

B   It must be made before the offer is accepted

C   It must be made by the offeror or a reliable third party   **(1 mark)**

48   Which of the following is correct in relation to social and domestic agreements?

A   It is presumed the parties did intend to create a legally binding contract

B   It is presumed that the parties did not intend to create a legally binding contract

C   It is irrelevant what the intention of the parties is   **(1 mark)**

49   Which of the following statements correctly describes express terms?

A   They are regarded as conditions

B   They are always in writing

C   They are terms that the parties have specifically agreed   **(1 mark)**

50   What is the principal effect of a counter-offer?

A   It destroys the original offer and replaces it with a new offer

B   It creates a binding contract based on the terms of the counter-offer

C   It creates a binding contract based on the terms of the original offer   **(1 mark)**

51   S offers to sell his car to B for £10,000 cash. At what point in time does the contract come into being?

A   When B accepts the offer

B   When B pays S the £10,000

C   When the agreement is written down

D   When the agreement is signed   **(2 marks)**

52   An offer was made by A to sell goods on the 1st April for £2,000. B the offeree telephoned A on the 5th April offering to pay £1,800 for the goods.

On the 8th April, A offered to sell the goods to C for £1,900, and C accepted this offer on the same day. On the 7th April, B sent a letter to A which was received on the 10th April agreeing to pay the £2,000 asking price for the goods.

Which one of the following is correct?

A   There is a contract between A and B created on the 7th April

B   There is a contract between A and B created on the 10th April

C   There is a contract between A and C

D   There is no contract created   **(2 marks)**

53   A coat was displayed in a shop window with a price tag attached which read £10. The price tag should have read £100. X who saw this went into the shop and demanded the coat for £10.

Which one of the following is correct?

A   As the window display is an offer X can demand the coat at £10.

B   The window display is merely an invitation to treat and the shopkeeper does not have to sell the coat to X.

C   The shopkeeper can refuse to sell the coat for £10, but cannot refuse to sell the coat to X for £100 if X was prepared to pay this sum.

D   The shopkeeper would be bound to sell the coat to any customer prepared to pay this £100.   **(2 marks)**

54   **In which of the following instances will a term NOT be incorporated into a business to business contract?**

A   Where a party signs the contract containing the term, whether they have read it or not.

B   Where the term is an exclusion clause under the Unfair Contract Terms Act 1977.

C   Where there is a course of dealing between the parties.

D   Where reasonable notice of the term is given but a contracting party remains unaware of its existence.   **(2 marks)**

55   **Which of the following statements about contract terms is NOT true?**

A   A contract term can be implied by a court on the ground of business efficacy.

B   A contract term can be implied by statute.

C   A contract term can be implied by a court on the basis of fairness between the parties.

D   A contract term can be implied by a court on the basis of trade custom.   **(2 marks)**

56   **Which of the following statements is NOT correct in relation to the determining of damages payable on breach of contract?**

A   The purpose of providing damages is to compensate the injured party.

B   Quantifying damages is determining the actual amount of the award to be made to the injured party.

C   The remoteness of damage issue is determined by considering the amount of damages the injured party reasonably expects on the basis of the contract breach and damages suffered.

D   An innocent party has a duty to mitigate their loss.   **2 marks)**

57 **What does the doctrine of privity of contract mean?**

    A   A contract is not legally binding if it is a private agreement

    B   Only the parties to a contract can enforce it

    C   The terms of a contract are primarily the concern of the parties to it

    D   An ambiguity in the contract will be interpreted against the party trying to avoid liability   **(2 marks)**

58 **In the event of a breach of contract, why is the difference between a condition and a warranty important?**

    A   It determines the measure of damages available to the innocent party

    B   It determines the type of damages available to the innocent party

    C   It determines the remedy available to the innocent party

    D   It determines whether or not the court will exercise its discretion to grant specific performance   **(2 marks)**

59 Robert's wife Kate expressed the wish that Robert, if he survived her, should have the use of her house. After Kate's death her executor agreed to allow Robert to occupy the house (i) because of Kate's wishes and (ii) on the payment by Robert of £24 per year.

Robert seeks to enforce this agreement and the executor wishes to avoid it in order to sell the house.

What is the legal position?

    A   Robert can enforce the agreement on the basis of his deceased wife's wishes.

    B   Robert cannot enforce the agreement because the promise to pay is not consideration.

    C   Robert can enforce the agreement because the promise of £24 per year provides consideration for it.

    D   Robert cannot enforce the agreement because £24 per year is not sufficient consideration.   **(2 marks)**

60 **In the context of contract law, which of the following is the correct limitation period for contracts (other than those made by deed)?**

    A   3 years

    B   6 years

    C   9 years

    D   15 years   **(2 marks)**

61 Paul has just agreed to sell a piece of land to his friend Martin.

Which of the following statements is correct?

    A   The contract is not enforceable as it is an agreement made between friends

    B   For the contract to enforceable, it can be in any form

    C   For the contract to be enforceable, the terms must be set out in writing

    D   For the contract to be enforceable, the Paul and Martin must be over 21 years old   **(2 marks)**

62 In the context of contract law, persons without capacity may have limitations on their power to contract.

Which of the following do/does NOT have capacity to contract?

(1) Persons under the age of eighteen years

(2) Persons of unsound mind

(3) Persons who are over the age of sixty five years

A (1) and (2) only

B (2) and (3) only

C (2) only

D (1), (2) and (3) **(2 marks)**

63 Nick verbally agrees to rob his friend's neighbour in return for £500.

In the context of contract law, which of the following statements is true?

A The contract is illegal, and therefore not valid

B The contract must be in writing for it to be enforceable

C Contracts made between friends are never legally binding

D The contract is enforceable if Nick is found not guilty of robbery **(2 marks)**

64 **In the context of contract law, which of the following statements is/are true?**

(1) An offer can be any form – oral, written or by conduct.

(2) An offer is not effective until has been communicated to the offeree.

(3) An offer can be made to a particular person, to class of persons, or certain instances to the whole world.

A (1) and (2) only

B (2) and (3) only

C (1) only

D (1), (2) and (3) **(2 marks)**

65 George sees a television for sale in the window of a shop, with a sign attached stating 'LIMITED OFFER PRICE £50'

This is an example of which of the following?

A An invitation to treat

B A valid offer

C A mere puff or boast

D A mere statement of selling price **(2 marks)**

66   Bobby sees a diamond ring in the display cabinet of a local jewellery shop, with a price tag of £25. When Bobby tried to buy the ring, the shop assistant informed him this was an error and the correct price is £2,500.

   Which of the following statements is correct?

   A   There is a binding contract for the ring at a price of £25

   B   There is a binding contract for the ring at a price of £25,000

   C   There is no contract since the ring on display is an invitation to treat

   D   There is no contract because an honest mistake has been made   **(2 marks)**

67   In contract law, once an offer has been terminated, it cannot be accepted.

   Which of the following does NOT terminate an offer?

   A   A request for further information

   B   Revocation by the offeror

   C   Lapse of reasonable time

   D   Rejection by the offeree   **(2 marks)**

68   **In the context of contract law, which of the following statements is/are true?**

   (1)   An offer can be in any form – oral, written or by conduct.

   (2)   An offer is terminated by rejection.

   (3)   An offer can be terminated after acceptance.

   A   (1) and (2) only

   B   (2) and (3) only

   C   (1) only

   D   (1), (2) and (3)   **(2 marks)**

69   In the context of contract law, an offer is terminated by revocation.

   Which of the following statements is/are true?

   (1)   Revocation can be made at any time prior to acceptance, even if the there is an agreement to keep the offer open.

   (2)   Revocation must be communicated to the offeree.

   (3)   Revocation can be communicated by ANY third party.

   A   (1) and (2) only

   B   (1) and (3) only

   C   (1) only

   D   (1), (2) and (3)   **(2 marks)**

70 In the context of contract law, which one of the following statements is NOT correct?

A   Acceptance must be unqualified and unconditional

B   Acceptance can be oral, written or by conduct

C   As a general principle, acceptance is not effective until it is communicated

D   Acceptance can be terminated by revocation   **(2 marks)**

71 The postal rule is an exception to the principle that acceptance must be communicated.

Which of the following is/are requirements for the postal rule to apply?

(1)   The letter must be received by the offeror

(2)   The letter must be properly stamped, addressed and posted

(3)   Accepting by post is a reasonable method of communication

A   (1) and (2) only

B   (2) and (3) only

C   (2) only

D   (1), (2) and (3)   **(2 marks)**

72 Stephen posted a letter of acceptance to Martin on 3rd December. On the 5th December Martin emailed Stephen to withdraw the offer. On the 6th December Martin received Stephen's letter of acceptance.

Which of the following statements best describes this situation?

A   There is NO contract. Martin has successfully revoked his offer by email prior to acceptance

B   There is NO contract. Acceptance in writing is not a valid form of acceptance

C   There is a contract on 3rd December

D   There is a contract on 6th December   **(2 marks)**

73 All simple contracts must be supported by consideration from each party.

Which of the following statements is/are correct?

(1)   Consideration must be sufficient

(2)   Consideration must be adequate

(3)   Past consideration is valid consideration.

A   (1) and (2) only

B   (1) and (3) only

C   (1) only

D   (1), (2) and (3)   **(2 marks)**

74 As a general rule, merely performing an existing legal duty is not sufficient consideration in contract law.

Which of the following is/are EXCEPTIONS to this rule?

(1) Where the consideration offered goes above and beyond existing legal duties.

(2) Where performing existing duties confers a benefit of a practical nature on the other party.

(3) Where the doctrine of promissory estoppel applies.

A (1) and (2) only

B (1) and (3) only

C (1) only

D (1), (2) and (3) **(2 marks)**

75 In contract law, the 'part-payment problem' refers to the general rule that payment of a smaller sum does not discharge a debt of a greater amount.

Which of the following is NOT an exception to this rule?

A Where payment is made by a third party

B Where there is accord and satisfaction

C Where the equitable doctrine of promissory estoppel applies

D Where both parties agree to a lower sum in full and final settlement **(2 marks)**

76 **According to common law, an EXCLUSION CLAUSE can be incorporated into a contract in which of the following ways?**

(1) By signature of the contract.

(2) By way of a notice.

(3) By way of previous dealings.

A (1) and (2) only

B (1) and (3) only

C (1) only

D (1), (2) and (3) **(2 marks)**

77 **In the context of contract law, which one of the following statements is NOT true?**

A A condition is an important term going to the root of the contract

B Breach of a condition can result in damages, or discharge, or both

C A warranty is less important term, merely incidental to main purpose of the contract

D Breach of a warranty can result in damages, or discharge, or both **(2 marks)**

78   John verbally agreed to sell his car to his brother for £3,000. Subsequently John changed his mind and decided to keep the car.

Which of the following statements is true?

A   John can be sued for breach of contract

B   There is no binding contract because the agreement was only verbal

C   There is no binding contract because this is an example of a domestic or social agreements

D   There is no binding contract because there is no valid consideration.   **(2 marks)**

79   In contract law, an exclusion clause is a term that seeks to exclude or limit a party's liability for breach of contract

Which of the following statements is correct?

A   The clause must meet the common law rules only

B   The clause must meet the statutory rules only

C   The clause must meet both the common law rules and the statutory rules   **(1 mark)**

80   Adam has a contract with Colin. Four weeks prior to the agreed completion date, Colin telephone's Adam out of courtesy to say he has double-booked and will be unable to carry out the work as agreed.

Which of the following statements is true?

A   Colin has committed an actual breach of contract

B   Colin has committed an express anticipatory breach of contract

C   Colin has committed an implied anticipatory breach of contract

D   Colin has not committed a breach of contract   **(2 marks)**

81   In the context of contract law, which of the following is a common law remedy for breach of contract?

A   Damages

B   Specific performance

C   Injunction

D   Rescission   **(2 marks)**

82   A judge orders a defendant to perform their contractual obligations as agreed.

In the context of contract law, which of the following is this example of?

A   Damages

B   Rescission of contract

C   Injunction

D   Specific performance   **(2 marks)**

83 A contract contains a term which states a fixed sum is payable in the event of breach. The sum is a genuine pre-estimate of the expected loss.

Which of the following is this an example of?

A   Liquidated damages

B   Penalty clause

C   Unliquidated damages

D   Equitable remedy   **(2 marks)**

84 Paul contracts with Green Ltd to landscape his garden for £1,500. The nearest alternative quote for the work was £2,200 from Eden Ltd. Before the due date for performance, Green Ltd contact Paul to say they can no longer do the work.

Which of the following damages can Paul claim for this breach of contract?

(1)   Financial compensation of £2,200

(2)   Financial compensation of £700.

A   (1) only

B   (2) only

C   Both (1) and (2)

D   Neither (1) or (2)   **(2 marks)**

85 Tabitha cleaned Zoe's house for a week while she was away and then demanded payment on Zoe's return.

Which of the following is correct?

A   Zoe does not have to pay Tabitha anything

B   Zoe should pay Tabitha the going rate for a cleaner

C   Zoe should at least pay Tabitha £1 for the services

D   A contract exists and Tabitha can sue Zoe for damages   **(2 marks)**

86 **Which of the following statement/s is/are correct in relation to damages?**

(1)   The claimant must take reasonable steps to mitigate their loss.

(2)   A notional deduction will not be made to reflect taxation.

A   (1) only

B   (2) only

C   Both (1) and (2)

D   Neither (1) or (2)   **(2 marks)**

87 Tan writes to Yun stating that he will sell his car to him for £10,000. At the same time, Yun writes to Tan stating that he will buy his car for £10,000.

Which of the following TWO statements apply to this situation?

A There is a binding agreement due to the postal rule

B There is a collateral contract

C Tan's letter to Yun constitutes an offer

D There is neither an agreement nor a contract **(2 marks)**

88 **Which of the following statements as regards an acceptance of an offer 'subject to contract' is true?**

A It binds the offeror

B It binds neither party

C It binds both parties **(1 mark)**

89 Jo promises to pay a reward for the return of her lost phone. Mia finds the phone and returns it to Jo.

Which of the following types of consideration has Mia provided?

A Executed consideration

B Executory consideration

C Past consideration

D Insufficient consideration **(2 marks)**

90 **Which of the following describes a pre-contractual statement which does NOT form a term of a contract but induces the contract?**

A A condition

B A warranty

C A representation

D An innominate term **(2 marks)**

91 **A breach of a contractual warranty enables the injured party to do which of the following?**

A To sue for damages only

B To sue for damages or terminate the contract

C To sue for damages and terminate the contract

D To terminate the contract only **(2 marks)**

92 **Which of the following actions is open to a party who has only partly performed work under a contract?**

   A   Quantum meruit

   B   Action for the price

   C   Damages

   D   Restitution   **(2 marks)**

93 **Where a business includes a term in a contract which excludes liability for death and personal injuries through negligence, which of the following states the effect of the term?**

   A   It is invalid

   B   It is invalid unless it is reasonable in the circumstances of the case

   C   It is valid only if specifically brought to the attention of the other party

   D   It is valid if it is clearly included in the contract terms   **(2 marks)**

94 **Which of the following is NOT a type of loss usually recoverable under the tort of negligence?**

   A   Injury

   B   Pure economic loss

   C   Damage to property   **(1 mark)**

95 **What is pure economic loss?**

   A   Financial loss that is caused by physical injury

   B   Financial loss that is not associated with physical injury or property damage

   C   Financial loss that is caused by damage to property   **(1 mark)**

96 **Which of the following correctly describes contributory negligence?**

   A   It is a partial defence

   B   It is a complete defence

   C   It is not a defence at all   **(1 mark)**

97 **Which of the following is NOT a situation where the courts have established that a duty of care exists?**

   A   Motorists owe a duty of care to pedestrians

   B   Manufacturers of products owe a duty of care to the ultimate users of those products

   C   An auditor of a company's accounts owes a duty of care to anyone who might read his report based on those accounts   **(1 mark)**

98   **Which of the following does NOT need to be shown by the claimant in order to succeed in an action for negligence?**

   A   That the defendant owed him a duty of care

   B   That the defendant was in breach of a duty of care

   C   That the claimant suffered injury, damage or loss as a result of a breach of a duty of care

   D   That the damage was not too remote   **(2 marks)**

99   **Which of the following is NOT considered in determining whether a duty of care exists?**

   A   Whether it is fair that the law should impose a duty on the defendant

   B   Whether the defendant intended to cause injury to the claimant

   C   Whether it was reasonably foreseeable that the claimant might suffer damage as a result of the defendant's actions

   D   Whether there is sufficient proximity between the parties   **(2 marks)**

100   **While taking driving lessons John drove negligently and injured his instructor. What will John's duty of care be?**

   A   The same as that owed by every driver

   B   That of any unqualified driver

   C   Assessed on the basis of John's specific experience and skill

   D   That which might reasonably be expected of a similarly inexperienced driver

                                                                              (2 marks)

101   **In negligence, to prove that damage arose from a breach of duty which of the following must be shown in addition to showing that the breach caused the damage?**

   A   The type of injury was reasonably foreseeable

   B   The extent of injury was reasonably foreseeable

   C   The particular injury was reasonably foreseeable

   D   Both the extent and type of injury was reasonably foreseeable   **(2 marks)**

102   **Which of the following does not need to be shown in an action for the tort of negligence?**

   A   That a duty of care was owed to the claimant by the defendant

   B   That there was breach of that duty of care

   C   That the defendant intended to harm the claimant

   D   That injury or damage was caused by the failure to exercise reasonable care

                                                                              (2 marks)

103 In relation to establishing a claim of negligence, which one of the following is NOT correct?

A There must be sufficient proximity between the wrongdoer and the injured party.

B The standard of care required is that expected by the reasonable person.

C The same level of care is owed both to adults and children.

D The level of care to be shown varies with the level of seriousness of the likely consequences of breach of duty. **(2 marks)**

104 Which of the following statements in relation to professional negligence is correct?

A A professional adviser can be liable to both the client who employs them and any other parties who they know will rely on information provided.

B A professional adviser can be liable to anyone who relies on information they provide.

C A professional adviser will be liable in negligence but not contract for any negligent advice provided.

D A professional adviser cannot be liable where the only form of damage resulting from negligent advice given is financial loss. **(2 marks)**

105 When determining whether a breach of duty has taken place, the courts will take into account a number of factors.

Which of the following is NOT a relevant factor?

A The seriousness of the injury

B The ease with which the damage sustained can be financially assessed

C The likelihood of injury

D The cost of precautions **(2 marks)**

106 In respect of audited accounts, to whom does an auditor owe a duty of care NOT to act negligently?

A The company only

B The shareholders only

C All stakeholders

D Anyone who purchases more shares in the company as a result of the accounts **(2 marks)**

107 Trina, a trainee accountant, was approached by John, the husband of Trina's colleague, Julie, at an office party. John asked her for some professional advice and flattered that he had asked her, Trina gave some advice. It later turned out her advice was flawed.

Is Trina liable of the resulting loss suffered by John?

A   Yes because she knows him and is responsible for the advice which she gives

B   Yes because she owes him a duty of care for which the standard is that of reasonable qualified accountant

C   No because she is only a trainee

D   No because the advice was not given in a professional context   **(2 marks)**

108 **Which of the following statement/s are true in relation to the defence of contributory negligence?**

(1)   The defendant must show that the claimant's conduct contributed to the incident that caused the damage he suffered.

(2)   The defendant must show that the claimant's conduct contributed to the damage which he suffered.

A   (1) only

B   (2) only

C   Both (1) and (2)

D   Neither (1) or (2)   **(2 marks)**

109 **Which of the following is the consequence when a patient signs a medical consent form before an operation?**

A   The patient gives up any right if action for any injury suffered

B   Any action for any injury suffered during the operation is limited to negligence

C   The level of any potential payment for any injury suffered is reduced   **(1 mark)**

110 Su had just passed her driving test when she negligently drove into a pedestrian.

What standard of care will Su be judged by?

A   The objective standard of a newly qualified driver, lack of experience will be taken into account

B   The objective standard of a competent driver, lack of experience will not be taken into account

C   The subjective standard of actual ability   **(1 mark)**

111 **Which of the following are owed a duty of care by auditors when preparing a company's audit report?**

A   A potential investor with no current holding

B   An existing shareholder looking to increase their holding

C   A company looking to make a takeover bid for the company

D   The company and the existing shareholders in the company as a body   **(2 marks)**

112 In relation to the tort of negligence, which TWO of the following criteria are required to establish the existence of a duty of care?

  (1) The claimant suffered a financial loss

  (2) The harm suffered was reasonably foreseeable

  (3) The relationship of proximity existed between the parties

  (4) The claimant did not consent to cause the injury suffered

  A (1) and (2)

  B (1) and (3)

  C (2) and (3)

  D (2) and (4)   (2 marks)

113 In relation to defences of the tort of negligence, which of the following is the consequence of a finding of volenti non fit injuria?

  A It removes the requirement to pay damages

  B It reverses the burden of proof as to who can claim damages

  C It increases the level of damages

  D It decreases the level of damages   (2 marks)

EMPLOYMENT LAW

114 Which of the following does NOT constitute a duty owed by an employee towards their employer under the common law?

  A A duty not to misuse confidential information

  B A duty to provide faithful service

  C A duty to obey all orders given to him by his employer   (1 mark)

115 Daniel has been working for Three Sixty Ltd for 18 months but his employment contract does NOT specify a notice period in the event of termination.

  What is the minimum period of notice to which he is entitled under the Employment Rights Act 1996?

  A At least 5 days

  B At least 1 week

  C At least 28 days

  C At least 1 month   (2 marks)

116 Which of the following is NOT valid for the dismissal of an employee?

  A Dishonesty

  B Wilful disobedience of a lawful order

  C Membership of a trade union   (1 mark)

117 Where can a claim for wrongful dismissal be brought?

A   The Employment Tribunal only

B   The County Court only

C   The County Court, the High Court, the Employment Tribunal   **(1 mark)**

118 What type of contract does an employee have?

A   A contract for service

B   A contract of service

C   A contract of services   **(1 mark)**

119 Breach of contract claims must normally be taken to an Employment Tribunal within what time period?

A   3 weeks of the effective date of termination

B   3 months of the effective date of termination

C   6 months of the effective date of termination   **(1 mark)**

120 When does a summary dismissal occur?

A   The parties agree to end the contract immediately

B   The employer terminates the contract with notice but no investigation

C   The employer terminates the contract without notice   **(1 mark)**

121 What is the minimum period of notice that an employee is entitled to after 12 years' service?

A   6 weeks

B   9 weeks

C   12 weeks   **(1 mark)**

122 Which of the following is correct in relation to where a constructive dismissal has been alleged?

A   It is unnecessary to show that the employer intended to repudiate the contract

B   It is necessary to show that the employer had a history of forcing employees out of their jobs

C   It is necessary to show that the employer intended to repudiate the contract **(1 mark)**

123 Which of the following is NOT a qualifying condition for unfair dismissal protection?

A   The claimant must be an employee

B   The claimant must have been provided with a letter stating the reason for the dismissal

C   The claimant must have been dismissed   **(1 mark)**

124 Anne works for E plc under a 4-year fixed-term contract of employment. At the end of the 4 years, E plc fails to renew the contract because Anne is pregnant.

Which of the following statements is /are correct?

(i) Anne will succeed in an action against E plc for wrongful dismissal,

(ii) Anne will succeed in an action against E plc for unfair dismissal.

A (i) only

B (ii) only

C Both (i) and (ii)

D Neither (i) nor (ii) **(2 marks)**

125 **Which of the following statement/s is/are correct?**

(i) An employer has an implied duty to behave reasonably and responsibly towards employees,

(ii) An employer has an implied duty to provide a reference.

A (i) only

B (ii) only

C Both (i) and (ii)

D Neither (i) nor (ii) **(2 marks)**

126 **When is an employee entitled to the written statement of prescribed particulars of employment?**

A Immediately on commencing employment

B Within one month of commencing employment

C Within two months of commencing employment

D After completing his trial period **(2 marks)**

127 **Which of the following statements in relation to unfair dismissal is NOT true?**

A It is automatically unfair to dismiss an employee for trade union activity

B It is automatically unfair to dismiss an employee who refuses to obey a reasonable instruction

C It is automatically unfair to dismiss an employee who becomes pregnant

D It is automatically unfair to dismiss an employee who complains on health and safety **(2 marks)**

128 **Which of the following statements is NOT true about wrongful dismissal?**

A It is a breach of contract

B It can be heard in both civil courts and employment tribunals

C It is a statutory right

D Liability is limited to the net pay for the maximum contractual-statutory notice period

(2 marks)

129 The courts can use a number of tests to determine if a person is employed or self-employed.

Which of the following is NOT one of the tests used to determine employment status?

A   The integration test

B   The economic reality test (or multiple test)

C   The factual test

D   The control test   **(2 marks)**

130 The distinction in status between employed and self-employed has a number of important consequences.

Which of the following statements is/are true?

(1)   Certain state benefits (e.g. statutory maternity pay) are only available to employees

(2)   An employee receives their pay gross (i.e. without deduction of income tax)

(3)   An employee receives statutory protection against unfair dismissal

A   (1) and (2) only

B   (1) and (3) only

C   (1) only

D   (1), (2) and (3)   **(2 marks)**

131 An employee has been informed by their employer that they are legally obliged to obey any lawful and reasonable orders.

Which of the following statements is true?

A   This is an example of a contractual term implied by common law

B   This is an example of a contractual term implied by statute

C   This is most likely to be an express contract term

D   The employer is incorrect, there is no legal obligation for an employee to obey lawful and reasonable orders   **(2 marks)**

132 Tom has been continuously employed by XYZ Ltd for 6 months.

Which of the following are available to Tom according to the Employment Rights Act 1996?

(1)   Wrongful dismissal

(2)   A written statement of particulars from his employer

(3)   Redundancy pay

A   (1) and (2) only

B   (1) and (3) only

C   (1) only

D   (1), (2) and (3)   **(2 marks)**

133 An employee resigns due the employer committing a serious breach of their employment contract.

Which of the following remedies is open to the employee?

A   Redundancy pay

B   No remedy is available to an employee who resigns

C   Constructive dismissal

D   Statutory sick pay   **(2 marks)**

134 **Which of the following is/are inadmissible reasons (automatically unfair) for dismissal?**

(1)   Pregnancy

(2)   Being convicted of a criminal offence

(3)   Whistleblowing

A   (1) and (2) only

B   (1) and (3) only

C   (1) only

D   (1), (2) and (3)   **(2 marks)**

135 Mark has been continuously employed by Stone Ltd for 18 months. He is dismissed, with notice, by his employer for requesting paid holiday leave.

Which of the following statements is true?

A   The reason for dismissal is automatically unfair, so Mark can bring action for unfair dismissal regardless of his length of employment

B   Mark cannot bring an action for unfair dismissal since he has not been in continuous employment for more than 2 years

C   Mark can claim statutory redundancy pay

D   Mark can claim constructive dismissal   **(2 marks)**

136 **In the context of employment law, which of the following statements is true?**

A   Terms can only be implied into employment contracts by judges under Common Law

B   Employees must obey ALL orders given by their employer

C   Employees must act with reasonable skill and care in the performance of their duties

D   Express contract terms always override implied contract terms   **(2 marks)**

137 **In the context of employment law, which of the following is NOT a remedy for unfair dismissal?**

A   Re-instatement

B   Re-engagement

C   Monetary compensation

D   A favourable employment reference   **(2 marks)**

138 In the context of employment law, there are circumstances where dismissal without notice is NOT 'wrongful'.

In which of the following circumstances does this apply?

(1) Both parties have mutually agreed to terminate the contract without notice

(2) The employee has received payment in lieu of notice

(3) The employee has committed a serious breach of contract

A (1) and (2) only

B (2) and (3) only

C (3) only

D (1), (2) and (3) **(2 marks)**

139 Stephen's contracted working hours were 7am – 3pm. When his employer attempted to force him to work night shifts instead, Stephen refused to do so and immediately resigned.

Which of the following is this an example of?

A Unfair dismissal

B Wrongful dismissal

C Constructive dismissal

D Redundancy **(2 marks)**

140 In the context of employment law, which of the following are required for an employee to bring action for unfair dismissal?

(1) Employee must be continuously employed for 2 years

(2) Employee must serve a grievance notice on the employer

(3) Employee must bring a claim to an employment tribunal within 3 months of dismissal

A (1) and (2) only

B (2) and (3) only

C (1) only

D (1), (2) and (3) **(2 marks)**

141 In the context of employment law, which of the following statements regarding wrongful dismissal is correct?

A Employee is dismissed without proper notice

B Employee resigns due the employer committing a serious breach of contract

C Employee is dismissed for unjustifiable reasons

D Employee is dismissed on the grounds of their religion **(2 marks)**

142 Terms are implied into employment contracts under common law (i.e. by judges), and statute.

Which of the following is NOT a term implied by common law?

A   Employers have a duty to provide a reference

B   Employers have a duty to provide a safe system of work

C   Employees have a duty to give honest and faithful service

D   Employees have a duty to obey lawful and reasonable orders   **(2 marks)**

143 Terms are implied into employment contracts under common law (i.e. by judges), and statute.

Which of the following is NOT a term implied by statute?

A   Employee has a right to a minimum level of pay

B   Employee has a right not to be unfairly dismissed

C   Employee has a right to four weeks paid leave a year

D   Employee has a right to be indemnified for any necessary expenses   **(2 marks)**

144 **Which of the following statements about contracts of employment is true?**

A   They can be made either orally or in writing

B   The must be made in writing

C   They must be evidenced in writing   **(1 mark)**

145 **Which of the following involves a summary dismissal in relation to a contract of employment?**

A   Both parties agree to end the contract immediately without notice

B   The employee breaks the contract without notice

C   The employer terminates the contract without notice   **(1 mark)**

146 **Statutory redundancy payment is calculated on the basis of which of the following?**

A   Length of service and pay only

B   Age and length of service only

C   Age, length of service and pay   **(1 mark)**

147 In a potential redundancy situation, an employee may lose the right to payment if they reject an offer of alternative employment within the business.

Which of the following will allow the employee to reject the employment offered and claim redundancy?

A   The alternative was suitable but the employee reasonably felt that it was not of the same status.

B   The alternative was suitable but the employee refused to consider it.

C   The alternative was suitable but the employee's grounds for refusing to accept it were unreasonable.   **(1 mark)**

148 Which TWO of the following are reasons for dismissal which must be justified as fair?

    (1)   Capability or qualifications of the employee

    (2)   Legal prohibitions relating to the employee

    (3)   Refusal of the employee to join a trade union

    (4)   Taking part in unofficial industrial action

    A   (1) and (2)

    B   (1) and (3)

    C   (2) and (3)

    D   (2) and (4)   **(2 marks)**

149 Which type of contract does an employee have?

    A   A contract for service

    B   A contract of service

    C   A contract for services

    D   A contract of services   **(2 marks)**

150 Which is the correct minimum period of notice an employee is entitled to after five years' service?

    A   One calendar month

    B   Five weeks

    C   Ten weeks

    D   Five calendar months   **(2 marks)**

THE FORMATION AND CONSTITUTION OF BUSINESS ORGANISATIONS

151 Which of the following must a public company have in order to trade?

    A   It must be listed on the London Stock Exchange

    B   It must have been issued with a certificate of incorporation

    C   It must have been issued with a certificate of Incorporation and a trading certificate

    (1 mark)

152 What type of resolution is required to alter a company's name?

    A   Ordinary resolution

    B   Special resolution

    C   Ordinary resolution with special notice   **(1 mark)**

153 **Which of the following must a public company limited by shares have?**

A   At least two directors and one shareholder

B   At least one director, one company secretary and two shareholders

C   At least two directors, one company secretary and one shareholder   **(1 mark)**

154 **Who does the articles of association of a company form a contract between?**

A   The shareholders and the directors in all respects

B   The shareholders and the company in all respects

C   The shareholders and the company in respect of shareholder rights only   **(1 mark)**

155 **Which of the following does NOT need to be submitted when registering a private company limited by shares?**

A   An application for registration

B   A statement of guarantee

C   A statement of compliance   **(1 mark)**

156 **Which of the following is NOT an example of a business organisation?**

A   A sole trader

B   An employee

C   A limited company   **(1 mark)**

157 **Which of the following is NOT a feature of a general partnership?**

A   The partners have unlimited liability

B   The partners have joint and severable liability

C   Only up to 20 partners are allowed   **(1 mark)**

158 **Which of the following is NOT a feature of a limited company?**

A   Directors are always immune from criminal prosecution

B   The shareholders have limited liability

C   The company has a separate legal personality   **(1 mark)**

159 **Who is the person on whose behalf an agent acts?**

A   Promoter

B   Preparer

C   Principal   **(1 mark)**

160 **Which of the following is an alternative name for apparent authority?**

A Ostensible authority

B Express authority

C Usual authority **(1 mark)**

161 Karishma owns a newsagent, runs it as the manager and employs Tessa as part-time help during the week. Karishma is fully liable for the business' debts.

What type of business does Karishma own?

A A partnership

B A company limited by guarantee

C A sole trader

D A company limited by shares **(2 marks)**

162 **What is the required nominal value of a public limited company's allotted share capital without which it cannot commence business?**

A £12,500

B £25,000

C £50,000 **(1 mark)**

163 **Within what period of time after the year end must a private company file its accounts with the Registrar?**

A Three months

B Six months

C Nine months **(1 mark)**

164 **To what extent is a member of a company limited by guarantee personally liable to contribute towards the company's debts?**

A He is liable to contribute towards all the company's debts at any time

B He is liable for all the company's debts on a winding up only

C His liability to contribute is limited to the amount he agreed to upon a winding up **(1 mark)**

165 **Which of the following is required to establish a general/ordinary partnership?**

A The partners obtain permission through Companies Act 2006

B The partners obtain permission from Companies House

C The partners simply agree to form the partnership **(1 mark)**

166 Irene entered into a pre-incorporation contract on behalf of Cosmo Ltd.

Which one of the following options correctly identifies the person who may enforce the contract and against whom it is enforceable?

A   By and against the company only

B   By and against Irene only

C   By the company and against Irene   **(1 mark)**

167 **Which of the following is NOT an example of how an agency relationship can come into existence?**

A   By express appointment

B   By ratification

C   Through an act of necessity

D   Through an act of a third party   **(2 marks)**

168 P delivers exclusive handbags to A, her agent, with instructions that they are NOT to be sold for less than £5,000 each. A sells a handbag to B for £5,000. B, believing that she has obtained a bargain, gives A a gift of £200.

What duty, if any, has A breached?

A   The duty to avoid a secret profit

B   The duty to act reasonably

C   The duty not to harm P's interests

D   No duty   **(2 marks)**

169 **The directors of a company are considering altering the company's Articles of Association. Who must the alteration be bona fide for the benefit of?**

A   Members and creditors

B   All current and future members

C   The company as a whole

D   The majority of the membership   **(2 marks)**

170 **Which of the following statements is/are correct?**

(i)   The partners in an ordinary partnership jointly own the firm's assets

(ii)   The shareholders in a company jointly own the company's assets

A   (i) only

B   (ii) only

C   Both (i) and (ii)

D   Neither (i) nor (ii)   **(2 marks)**

171 The Articles of Association of ABC Ltd provide that all disputes between ABC Ltd and its directors must be referred to arbitration. Del is a director of ABC Ltd and is in dispute with the company about late payment of his director's fees.

Which of the following is/are correct?

(i) Del is obliged by the Articles of Association to refer the dispute to arbitration whether or not he is a shareholder.

(ii) Del is obliged by the Articles of Association to refer the dispute to arbitration only if he is a shareholder.

A (i) only

B (ii) only

C Both (i) and (ii)

D Neither (i) nor (ii) **(2 marks)**

172 Immediately prior to the incorporation of Products Ltd, Roberts, one of its promoters, bought property in his own name from Suppliers Ltd. He later sold the property to Products Ltd at a large profit without disclosure.

To whom is Roberts liable in relation to this secret profit?

A Suppliers Ltd

B Products Ltd

C The promoters of Products Ltd

D The shareholders of Products Ltd **(2 marks)**

173 Which of the following must sign the Memorandum of Association of a company?

A The subscribers and all the directors

B The subscribers and at least one of the directors

C The subscribers and the company secretary

D The subscribers only **(2 marks)**

174 Popeye is the promoter of Spinach Ltd. He and his wife Olive are the first directors of the company. Popeye sold a plot of land he owned to the company making a profit of £20,000.

What is the legal position regarding the profit?

A Popeye may keep the profit in any event

B Popeye may keep the profit as long as it is disclosed to the board of directors

C Popeye may keep the profit as long as it is disclosed to the first shareholders of the company

D Popeye may not keep the profit under any circumstances **(2 marks)**

175 Which of the following are NOT bound to one another by the articles of association?

    A   The company to third parties

    B   Members to the company

    C   The company to members

    D   The company to directors   **(2 marks)**

176 In company law, what is meant by the term 'veil of incorporation'?

    A   A company is a separate legal entity to its shareholders and directors.

    B   A company has perpetual succession.

    C   A company pays corporation tax

    D   A company owns its own property   **(2 marks)**

177 A company is a separate legal entity to its shareholders and directors.

Which of the following are consequences of separate legal entity?

    (1)   A company is fully liable for its own debts

    (2)   A company owns its own property

    (3)   A company enters into contracts in its own name

    A   (1) and (2) only

    B   (1) and (3) only

    C   (2) and (3) only

    D   (1), (2) and (3)   **(2 marks)**

178 There are a number of important legal differences between unincorporated businesses (e.g. partnerships), and incorporated businesses (e.g. companies).

Which of the following are characteristics of a COMPANY?

    (1)   A company has perpetual succession

    (2)   A company is subject to the requirements of the Companies Act 2006.

    (3)   There is no separation of ownership and management in a company.

    A   (1) and (2) only

    B   (1) and (3) only

    C   (2) and (3) only

    D   (1), (2) and (3)   **(2 marks)**

179 A shareholder believes that one of the company directors has misapplied company assets and wishes to take legal action against the director.

Which of the following statements is true?

A   The shareholder can personally take legal action against the director.

B   A minimum of 5 shareholders is required to take legal action against the director

C   The shareholder cannot take legal action. Only the company is able to sue the director as it is the company that has suffered harm

D   The shareholder is forbidden from disclosing this due to confidentiality   **(2 marks)**

180 **In the context of company law, in which of the following circumstances has it been considered necessary to lift the veil of incorporation?**

(1)   Where a company is sham, established to help a party evade contractual obligations.

(2)   To identify the true nationality of a company.

(3)   Where a disqualified director participates in the management of a company.

A   (1) and (2) only

B   (1) and (3) only

C   (2) and (3) only

D   (1), (2) and (3)   **(2 marks)**

181 There are a number of important legal differences between companies and partnerships.

Which of the following statements is NOT true?

A   There no formality required to create a partnership.

B   Partnerships can create both fixed and floating charges as security for borrowing.

C   Partners in a partnership are personally liable for the debts of the firm.

D   Partnerships are not legally required to disclose their financial results to the general public   **(2 marks)**

182 There are a number of important legal differences between companies and partnerships.

Which of the following statements is NOT true?

A   Companies are created by a formal registration procedure

B   Companies are owned by shareholders, and managed by directors

C   Companies must legally disclose certain financial information to the general public

D   Companies may dissolve by agreement of the directors   **(2 marks)**

183 In the context of company law, which of the following statements are true?

(1) A private company can be limited or unlimited.

(2) A private company can be limited by shares or by guarantee.

(3) A public company can be limited by shares or by guarantee.

A (1) and (2) only

B (1) and (3) only

C (2) and (3) only

D (1), (2) and (3) **(2 marks)**

184 Which of the following is NOT a legal requirement of a public company?

A Name must end with 'plc' or 'public limited company'

B Must have a minimum of two directors

C Must have a company secretary

D In order to trade must have allotted shares of at least £25,000 **(2 marks)**

185 Tom is in the process of forming a company for his new business venture. He is keen to enter into pre-incorporation contracts but aware that he will be personally liable for any such contracts.

What steps can Tom take to overcome the problem of pre-incorporation contracts?

(1) Postpone finalising contracts until after the company is formed.

(2) Entering into an agreement of novation with all parties.

(3) Buying an 'off-the-shelf' company to trade with immediately.

A (1) and (2) only

B (1) and (3) only

C (2) and (3) only

D (1), (2) and (3) **(2 marks)**

186 In context of company registration, which of the following is NOT included in the Statement of Capital?

A The number of shares taken on formation

B Their aggregate nominal value

C The amount paid-up on each share

D A contact address for each subscriber **(2 marks)**

187 In company law, the name of a company must comply with strict rules.

Which of the following statements is NOT true?

A A company cannot have the same name as another company

B Permission is required from the Secretary of State to use certain words such as 'Royal', 'Chartered', 'National' etc

C A company's name cannot include words that are illegal or offensive

D All company names must end in 'Limited' or 'Ltd' **(2 marks)**

188 The articles of association form a company's internal constitution.

Which of the following statements is NOT true?

A There are no mandatory contents

B Articles of Association must be submitted as part of the company registration process

C The articles operate as a binding contract between individual members in their capacity as members

D Articles can usually be altered by a special resolution of members **(2 marks)**

189 In company law, the articles of association can usually be altered by a special resolution of members.

In what circumstances can articles NOT be altered by special resolution?

(1) Where the articles are entrenched.

(2) Where the alteration seeks to increase a member's liability to the company.

(3) Where the alteration is NOT in the bona fide interests of the company as a whole.

A (1) and (2) only

B (1) and (3) only

C (2) and (3) only

D (1), (2) and (3) **(2 marks)**

190 **In relation to the statutory books, returns and records of a company, which of the following statements is correct?**

A Records of resolutions and meetings must be kept for a minimum of 10 years.

B The annual confirmation statement contains details of fixed and floating charges created over the company's property.

C A company's registers are not available for public inspection. **(1 mark)**

191 **An agency relationship which is made retrospectively is referred to by which of the following terms?**

A Agency by estoppel

B Agency by ratification

C Agency by necessity **(1 mark)**

192 Which TWO of the following apply to shares of companies whose names end in 'Ltd'?

(1)   They may not be issued to non-members

(2)   They may not be offered to the public

(3)   They may not be transferred

(4)   They may not be traded on the stock exchange

A   (1) and (2)

B   (2) and (3)

C   (1) and (4)

D   (2) and (4)   (2 marks)

193 Which of the following must a private company ALWAYS have?

A   Shares

B   Limited liability

C   A company secretary

D   A registration certificate   (2 marks)

194 Which of the following exists as a separate legal entity from its members?

A   An ordinary partnership

B   A limited partnership

C   A limited liability partnership   (1 mark)

195 In relation to agency law, 'warrant of authority' is provided by which of the following?

A   The agent

B   The principal

C   The third party   (1 mark)

CAPITAL AND THE FINANCING OF COMPANIES

196 When a company sells its shares at a higher value than the nominal value what happens to the difference in value?

A   It is transferred into a share premium account

B   It is distributed to members as dividends

C   It is kept by the directors as a bonus   (1 mark)

197 What is the amount of the nominal share capital that has been paid for by the company members called?

A   Paid-up share capital

B   Issued share capital

C   Allotted share capital   (1 mark)

198 Which of the following is NOT a type of share of a company?

    A   Ordinary

    B   Special

    C   Preference   **(1 mark)**

199 Which of the following correctly describes a floating charge?

    A   It is on a class of current assets which can be identified

    B   It is on a class of assets which may change in the ordinary course of business

    C   It is on a class of assets, present or future, which may change in the ordinary course of business   **(1 mark)**

200 Which of the following statements is correct in relation to a private company wishing to reduce its share capital?

    A   It must pass an ordinary resolution

    B   It must pass a special resolution

    C   It does not need to pass a resolution   **(1 mark)**

201 Which of the following statements describes treasury shares?

    A   Shares issues by a public company to a creditor

    B   A company's own shares that it legitimately purchased out of distributable profit

    C   Shares held by a public company as an investment   **(1 mark)**

202 Which of the following statements describes a debenture?

    A   The registration document used to register a fixed or floating charge

    B   A document that records the terms of any loan

    C   A document that records the terms of any secured loan   **(1 mark)**

203 In relation to charges which of the following is correct?

    A   A private company cannot create charges

    B   A public company cannot create floating charges

    C   Both private and public companies may create fixed and floating charges   **(1 mark)**

204 Where a company legitimately purchases 10% of its own shares out of profit, what can it hold them as?

    A   Treasury shares

    B   Ordinary shares

    C   Preference shares   **(1 mark)**

205 **If a charge is created over property where must it be registered?**

    A   Companies Registry

    B   HMRC

    C   Land registry   **(1 mark)**

206 **Which of the following sources of company finance typically carries NO fixed entitlement to income?**

    A   Ordinary shares

    B   Preference shares

    C   Secured debentures

    D   Unsecured debentures   **(2 marks)**

207 **Which of the following sources of company finance is classed as 'equity' but typically carries NO voting rights?**

    A   Ordinary shares

    B   Preference shares

    C   Secured debentures

    D   Unsecured debentures   **(2 marks)**

208 **In the context of company finance, which of the following statements is true?**

    A   Fixed charges rank lower than floating charges on winding up

    B   Fixed charges rank lower than preference shares on winding up

    C   Fixed charges are security over a specific asset

    D   Fixed charges are security over a class of assets   **(2 marks)**

209 **In the context of company finance, which of the following are advantages of debentures?**

    (1)   Debentures carry no voting rights and therefore do not dilute control of existing shareholders.

    (2)   There are no restrictions on the company issuing debentures at a discount.

    (3)   The board of directors do not usually require authority of shareholders to issue debentures.

    A   (1) and (2) only

    B   (1) and (3) only

    C   (2) and (3) only

    D   (1), (2) and (3)   **(2 marks)**

210 In the context of company finance, which of the following are disadvantages of debentures?

(1) Debentures carry no voting rights and therefore do not dilute control of existing shareholders.

(2) Interest must be paid to debenture holders irrespective of whether there are profits available.

(3) High levels of debt will adversely affect a company's share price.

A (1) and (2) only

B (1) and (3) only

C (2) and (3) only

D (1), (2) and (3) **(2 marks)**

211 A company wishes to raise finance by issuing new shares to existing shareholders for an amount slightly less than their current market value?

This is an example of which of the following?

A Bonus issue

B Rights issue

C Issue at a discount

D Issue at nominal value **(2 marks)**

212 In company law, directors require authority to make a share issue.

Which of the following statements is NOT true?

A Authority may be given in the articles of association

B Authority may be given by passing an ordinary resolution

C The authority must state the maximum number of shares to be issued

D The maximum expiry date for the authority is TWO years **(2 marks)**

213 In the context of a company issuing shares, which one of the following is FORBIDDEN by the Companies Act 2006?

A Issuing shares at a premium to nominal value

B Issuing shares at a discount to nominal value

C Issuing partly paid shares

D Issuing bonus shares **(2 marks)**

214 In company law, a premium received on the issue of new shares must be credited to a 'share premium reserve'.

Which of the following can the share premium reserve NOT be used for?

A Writing off expenses of the share issue

B Writing off any commission paid on the share issue

C Issuing bonus shares

D Funding dividends to shareholders **(2 marks)**

224 The category of treasury shares comes into existence under which of the following circumstances?

    A   They are issued as such by a private company

    B   They are issued as such by a public company

    C   They are purchased as such by the exchequer

    D   They are purchased as such by a private or public company   **(2 marks)**

MANAGEMENT, ADMINISTRATION AND REGULATION OF COMPANIES

225 Ceres plc last held an AGM on 31 October 2007.

    When must the company hold its next annual general meeting (AGM)?

    A   31 October 2009

    B   31 December 2009

    C   Within 6 month period after the accounting reference date

    D   Within 9 month period after the accounting reference date   **(2 marks)**

226 For which of the following is an ordinary resolution of the shareholders sufficient authority?

    A   To amend a private company's articles

    B   To change a private company's name

    C   To give directors authority to issue new shares   **(1 mark)**

227 What is the quorum for a general meeting of a registered company?

    A   Two persons being members or proxies for members

    B   Three persons being members or proxies for members

    C   Two persons being members   **(1 mark)**

228 Where a person is held out by a company as a director and performs the duties of a director without being validly appointed, what is that person deemed to be?

    A   A de facto director

    B   A shadow director

    C   An executive director   **(1 mark)**

229 When is shorter notice than that required for an AGM of a plc permitted?

    A   With a minimum member support of 75%

    B   With a minimum member support of 90%

    C   With 100% member support   **(1 mark)**

230 What percentage of support is required to pass a written ordinary resolution in a private limited company?

    A   100%

    B   95%

    C   50%+   **(1 mark)**

231 Which of the following is NOT a type of company director?

    A   A supreme director

    B   An executive director

    C   A shadow director   **(1 mark)**

232 What is the minimum age of a director as required by Companies Act 2006?

    A   16

    B   18

    C   21   **(1 mark)**

233 To whom does a director owe their statutory duties to?

    A   The members

    B   The board of directors

    C   The company as a whole   **(1 mark)**

234 Which of the following describes a director with day to day responsibility for running a company?

    A   Chairman of the Board

    B   President

    C   Managing Director   **(1 mark)**

235 Which of the following is NOT a type of meeting?

    A   Annual general meeting

    B   General meeting

    C   Special meeting   **(1 mark)**

236 Which of the following statements in relation to auditors is correct?

    A   An auditor must be a member of a recognised supervisory body

    B   Only individuals and not firms can act as an auditor

    C   An auditor cannot be removed until their term of office has expired   **(1 mark)**

237   Gulliver Ltd has recently dismissed one of its directors. Gulliver Ltd wishes to pay Joe compensation for loss of office.

Who must approve this payment?

A   The board of directors

B   HMRC

C   The creditors

D   The shareholders in a general meeting   **(2 marks)**

238   **Which of the following statements are true?**

(i)   The statutory duty of a director to disclose any interest that he has in a proposed transaction or arrangement with the company does not apply to shadow directors.

(ii)   A director may not exercise his powers except for the purpose for which they were conferred.

A   (i) only

B   (ii) only

C   Both (i) and (ii)

D   Neither (i) or (ii)   **(2 marks)**

239   Steven and his fellow directors Marcus and Tom each own 100 of the 300 shares in Simple Pies Ltd. Under the articles of association, where a resolution is proposed to remove a director, that director is entitled to three votes per share. Marcus and Tom vote to remove Steven but when a poll is taken, Steven defeats the resolution by 300 votes to 200.

Which of the following best describes the legal position?

A   Steven has not been removed because the weighted voting rights have been validly given and validly exercised.

B   Steven has been removed because the article giving weighted voting rights contravenes the Companies Act 2006 which enables a director to be removed on the passing of an ordinary resolution with special notice.

C   Steven has not been validly removed because the articles would effectively mean that a director could never be removed.

D   Steven has been validly removed because voting should not have been conducted by a poll on a resolution to remove a director.   **(2 marks)**

240   **Which TWO of the following are statutory duties of a director?**

A   To promote the success of the company

B   To promote the relationship between directors and employees

C   To declare trading losses to members

D   To declare an interest in an existing transaction or arrangement   **(2 marks)**

241 Rebecca is appointed director of Blue Ltd, and given ultimate control over the day-to-day management of the company.

In the context of company law, what is Rebecca considered to be?

A   Managing director

B   Shadow director

C   Non-executive director

D   De-facto director   **(2 marks)**

242 Margaret is appointed by a director of Peach Ltd to attend and vote for them at board meetings when they are personally unable to attend.

In the context of company law, which of the following types of director is Margaret classified as?

A   Chief executive officer

B   Alternate director

C   Non-executive director

D   Shadow director   **(2 marks)**

243 The Company Directors (Disqualification) Act 1986 identifies distinct categories of conduct which may give rise to a disqualification order being made.

Which of the following are NOT grounds for disqualification under the Act?

A   Persistent breaches of the Companies Act 2006

B   Unfitness to manage a company

C   Participation in wrongful trading

D   Committing a criminal offence   **(2 marks)**

244 **In company law, what period of notice is required by the use of the term special notice when removing a director from office?**

A   14 days

B   21 days

C   28 days

D   31 days   **(2 marks)**

245 **In company law, which of the following is NOT a statutory duty of directors?**

A   Duty to act within their powers

B   Duty to exercise independent judgement

C   Duty to avoid conflicts of interest

D   Duty to protect shareholder value   **(2 marks)**

246 A director is in breach of their statutory duties.

Which of the following statements is NOT true?

A   Directors owe their duties to the company as a whole, not to individual members.

B   The director may be required to make good any loss suffered by the company.

C   Any property taken by the director from the company can be recovered from them if it is still in their possession.

D   Breach of statutory duties is grounds for disqualification under the Company Directors (Disqualification) Act 1986.   **(2 marks)**

247 In relation to company secretaries, which of the following statements is NOT true?

A   All companies must have a company secretary.

B   There are no statutory duties of company secretary.

C   A company secretary has the apparent authority to bind the company in contracts of an administrative nature.

D   A company secretary requires express (actual) authority from the board to bind the company in commercial contracts.   **(2 marks)**

248 Which of the following applies to the concept of enlightened shareholder value?

A   It is the price shares can be expected to raise if they were to be sold

B   It is the yardstick for assessing the performance of directors' duties

C   It is the standard of behaviour expected of shareholders in general meetings
                                                                                (1 mark)

249 Which of the following statements regarding the age limits for serving as a director in a public limited company is true?

A   Minimum age 16 years and no maximum age

B   Minimum age 21 years and no maximum age

C   Minimum age 21 years and maximum age 75 years

D   Minimum age 16 years and maximum age 75 years   **(2 marks)**

INSOLVENCY LAW

250 When a director makes a Declaration of Solvency before a members' voluntary liquidation, for how many months are they stating that the company will be able to pay its debts?

A   3 months

B   6 months

C   12 months   **(1 mark)**

251 When is a company deemed to be unable to pay its debts for the purposes of a compulsory liquidation?

    A   Where a creditor is owed at least £250

    B   Where a creditor is owed at least £500

    C   Where a creditor is owed at least £750   (1 mark)

252 Which of the following persons or bodies can petition to the court for a compulsory liquidation?

    A   The company itself

    B   Any creditor

    C   Any director   (1 mark)

253 When a liquidator is appointed, he becomes the agent of which of the following?

    A   The members

    B   The creditors

    C   The company   (1 mark)

254 On a compulsory winding up of a company, who will the court usually appoint?

    A   The auditor of the company

    B   The Official Receiver

    C   A qualified insolvency practitioner   (1 mark)

255 When a company goes into a creditors voluntary winding up, what is the maximum number of persons that can be appointed to serve on the Liquidation Committee?

    A   5

    B   8

    C   10

    D   12   (2 marks)

256 When a company goes into a creditors' voluntary winding up, who ultimately has the right to appoint the liquidator?

    A   Ordinary shareholders

    B   Preference shareholders

    C   Creditors

    D   Directors   (2 marks)

257 Which of the following is NOT a ground for compulsory winding up under the Insolvency Act 1986?

    A   A public company has not been issued with a trading certificate within a year of incorporation

    B   The company has not paid a dividend during the last two years

    C   It is just and equitable to wind up the company

    D   The company has passed a special resolution to be wound up by the court   **(2 marks)**

258 Which of the following is a preferential creditor when a company goes into liquidation?

    A   Arrears of holiday pay due to employees

    B   Money owed to HMRC for PAYE deductions

    C   Money owed to utilities providers

    D   Money owed to a builder for a recent refurbishment   **(2 marks)**

259 Which of the following ranks lowest in a liquidation?

    A   Trade creditors

    B   Fixed charge holder

    C   Floating charge holder

    D   Employees for unpaid wages   **(2 marks)**

260 Which of the following CANNOT appoint an administrator directly?

    A   The court

    B   The holder of a qualifying floating charge over the company's assets

    C   The company itself

    D   A creditor who is owed £800   **(2 marks)**

261 Which of the following is NOT an immediate and automatic consequence of administration?

    A   All employees are made redundant

    B   Any outstanding petition for winding up is dismissed

    C   No resolution may be passed to wind up the company

    D   The directors still continue in office   **(2 marks)**

262 Which of the following statements regarding an administrator are correct?

    (i)   An administrator is the company's agent

    (ii)   An administrator must act in the best interests of all the company's creditors

    A   (i) only

    B   (ii) only

    C   Both (i) and (ii)

    D   Neither (i) or (ii)   **(2 marks)**

263 An administrator can pay out monies to which of the following without court approval?

(i) Secured creditors

(ii) Preferential creditors

(iii) Unsecured creditors

A (i) and (ii)

B (i) and (iii)

C (ii) and (iii)

D (i) only **(2 marks)**

264 Where directors make a false statement of solvency prior to a members' voluntary liquidation, which of the following have they committed under the relevant legislation?

A A breach of criminal law with criminal penalties

B A breach of civil law with criminal penalties

C A breach of civil law with civil liability

D A breach of both civil and criminal law with liabilities under both **(2 marks)**

265 Which of the following requires court approval before the appointment of an administrator?

A Creditors

B Holders of floating charges

C The directors of the company

D The company itself **(2 marks)**

266 Which of the following is NOT an automatic consequence of a compulsory winding up order against a public limited company?

A Transfers if shareholdings are suspended

B Liquidation is deemed to start on the date of the issuing of the order

C Directors cease to exercise any management power

D Employees are immediately dismissed **(2 marks)**

267 In which procedure does a liquidation committee operate?

(1) Compulsory liquidation

(2) A members' voluntary liquidation

(3) A creditors' voluntary liquidation

(4) Administration

A (1) and (2)

B (2) and (4)

C (1) and (3)

D (3) and (4) **(2 marks)**

CORPORATE FRAUDULENT AND CRIMINAL BEHAVIOUR

268 **What type of action can fraudulent trading give rise to?**

    A   Civil action only

    B   Criminal action only

    C   Both civil and criminal action   **(1 mark)**

269 **Which of the following are able to enter into a deferred prosecution agreement?**

    A   Individuals only

    B   Commercial organisations only

    C   Both individuals and commercial organisations   **(1 mark)**

270 **When a person suspects another of money laundering, to whom should they report this suspicion to?**

    A   Financial Conduct Authority

    B   National Crime Agency

    C   Department of Business, Innovation and Skills   **(1 mark)**

271 **In relation to money laundering, when monies take on the appearance of coming from a legitimate source, what is this is known as?**

    A   Placement

    B   Layering

    C   Integration   **(1 mark)**

272 **What is a valid defence against the corporate offence of failing to prevent bribery?**

    A   Having adequate procedures in place, based on a risk assessment

    B   Lack of knowledge of the offence

    C   The offence was committed by a temporary member of staff   **(1 mark)**

273 **What type of law is market abuse a breach of?**

    A   Criminal law only

    B   Civil law only

    C   Criminal and civil law   **(1 mark)**

274 **What is it necessary to establish to convict someone of fraudulent trading?**

    A   That the directors had dishonest intent

    B   That the directors were not shadow directors

    C   That the shareholders suffered a loss   **(1 mark)**

275 **What are the phases of money laundering?**

(i)   Integration

(ii)   Layering

(iii)   Adjustment

(iv)   Placement

A   (i), (ii) and (iii)

B   (i) and (ii) only

C   (ii) and (iii) only

D   (i), (ii) and (iv)   **(2 marks)**

276 **Which of the following are characteristics of inside information?**

(i)   The information relates to particular securities or issuer of securities

(ii)   The information is specific or precise

(iii)   The information is not public

(iv)   If made public, the information would affect the price of the security

A   (i) and (iii) only

B   (i) only

C   (ii) and (iii) only

D   (i), (ii), (iii) and (iv)   **(2 marks)**

277 **Which of the following is a corporate bribery offence?**

A   Bribing an individual

B   Receiving a bribe

C   Bribing a public foreign official

D   Failure to prevent bribery   **(2 marks)**

278 **Which of the following statements is correct?**

An action for wrongful trading can be brought:

(i)   Regardless of whether the company is solvent or not

(ii)   Against directors and shadow directors only

A   (i) only

B   (ii) only

C   Both (i) and (ii)

D   Neither (i) and (ii)   **(2 marks)**

279 In relation to wrongful trading, the standard against which the conduct of directors will be assessed is which of the following?

    A   Purely subjective, depending on the actual skill of the director

    B   Purely objective, depending on what is expected of a director in that position

    C   A mixture of subjective and objective but only to increase potential liability

    D   A mixture of subjective and objective but only to reduce potential liability   **(2 marks)**

Section 2

MULTI-TASK QUESTIONS

THE LAW OF OBLIGATIONS

280 AMY AND BEN (A) (PBE)

In January 2009, Amy started a business as an independent website designer. To give her a start in her career, her brother Ben, who ran a retail business, said he would give her £1,000 if she updated his business website.

However, by the time Amy had completed the project her design business had become a huge success and she had lots of other clients. When Ben discovered how successful Amy's business had become he felt that he should not be asked to pay for the work which Amy had done.

Ben said he would not pay anything as he had only offered the work to help his sister out.

Required:

(a) Explain the principle of intention to create a legal relationship in relation to domestic and social agreements. **(2 marks)**

(b) Explain whether Amy can take legal action against Ben. **(4 marks)**

(Total: 6 marks)

281 ARTI (A) (PBE)

In January 2008 Arti entered in a contractual agreement with Bee Ltd to write a study manual for an international accountancy body's award. It was a term of the contract that the text should be supplied by 30 June 2008 so that it could be printed in time for September. By 30 May, Arti had not yet started on the text and indeed he had written to Bee Ltd stating that he was too busy to write the text.

Bee Ltd was extremely perturbed by the news, especially as it had acquired the contract to supply all of the accountancy body's study manuals and had already incurred extensive preliminary expenses in relation to the publication of the new manual.

Required:

(a) State the meaning of anticipatory breach of contract. **(2 marks)**

(b) Explain whether Bee Ltd can make a claim for specific performance against Arti. **(2 marks)**

(c) Identify which remedy would be appropriate for Bee Ltd to claim. **(2 marks)**

(Total: 6 marks)

282   AMY AND BRY (A) (PBE)

In January 2010 Ami took over an old warehouse with the intention of opening an art gallery. As the warehouse had to be converted, Ami entered into a contract with Bry to do the conversion for £5,000. Bry received an initial payment of £1,000 and agreed to have the work completed on 31 March, as the art gallery had to be ready for its first exhibition on 1 May.

At the end of February, Bry told Ami that he would not complete the work in time unless she agreed to increase his payment by a further £1,000. Ami agreed to pay the increased sum in order to ensure that the job was done on time.

However, on completion of the work on time Ami refused to make the additional payment to Bry beyond the original contractual price.

Required:

(a)   Explain whether the performance of existing contractual duties can provide consideration for a new promise.   **(2 marks)**

(b)   Explain whether Bry can enforce Ami's promise to pay the additional sum. **(4 marks)**

(Total: 6 marks)

283   BILD LTD (A) (CBE)

Astride entered into a contract with Bild Ltd to construct a wall around the garden of a house she had just purchased. The wall was to be three metres high to block out a view of a rubbish tip.

Bild Ltd finished the wall on 25 May. However when Astride came to examine it for the first time she found that it was only 2.50 metres high and that the rubbish tip was still visible from the top of her garden. The cost of making the wall meet the required height is £2,000.

Task 1   **(2 marks)**

Which TWO of the following statements explain the purpose of awarding damages for breach of contract?

*   **They are a punishment for the party in breach**
*   **They compensate the injured party for any financial loss**
*   **They put the parties in the position they were in before the contract was formed**
*   **They put the parties in the position they would have been in had the contract been performed**

Task 2   **(2 marks)**

Which TWO of the following statements explain how damages could be measured in a building contract?

*   **It would be the difference in value between the building as it has been completed and its value if it had been properly completed**
*   **It would be the cost of completing the work to an industry standard specification**
*   **It would be the cost of completing the work to the required specification regardless of the cost**
*   **It would be the cost of completing the work to the required specification unless the cost of remedying the defects are disproportionate to the difference in value between what was supplied and what was ordered**

Task 3 (2 marks)

Which of the following remedies would Astride claim for?

- Specific performance
- Nominal damages
- Injunction
- Damages of £2,000

284 ALI (A) (CBE)

Ali is an antique dealer and one Saturday in November 2007 he put a vase in the window of his shop with a sign which stated 'exceptional piece of 19th century pottery – on offer for £500'.

Ben happened to notice the vase as he walked past the shop and thought he would like to have it. Unfortunately, as he was late for an important meeting, he could not go into the shop to buy it, but as soon as his meeting was finished he wrote to Ali agreeing to buy the vase for the stated price of £500. The letter was posted at 11:30 am.

Just before closing time at 5 pm. Di came into Ali's shop and she also offered £400 for the vase. This time Ali agreed to sell the vase at that price and Di promised to return the following Monday with the money.

On the Monday morning Ali received the letter from Ben before Di could arrive to pay and collect the vase.

Task 1 (2 marks)

Which TWO of the following statements are correct?

- An offer must be in writing
- An offer can be in any form
- An offer must be communicated to the offeree
- A statement of selling price constitutes an offer

Task 2 (2 marks)

Which TWO of the following statements are correct?

- The shop window sign and display is an offer
- The shop window sign and display is an invitation to treat
- Ben's letter to Ali is an offer
- Ben's letter to Ali is acceptance

Task 3 (2 marks)

Which TWO of the following statements are correct?

- There is a contract between Ali and Ben
- There is no contract between Ali and Ben
- There is a contract between Ali and Di
- There is no contract between Ali and Di

285 ALVIN (A) (PBE)

Alvin runs a business selling expensive cars. Last Monday he mistakenly placed a notice on one car indicating that it was for sale for £5,000 when in fact its real price was £25,000. Bert later noticed the sign and, recognising what a bargain it was, immediately indicated to Alvin that he accepted the offer and would take the car for the indicated amount. Alvin, however, told Bert that there had been a mistake and that the true price of the car was £25,000. Bert insisted that he was entitled to get the car at the lower price, and when Alvin would not give it to him at that price Bert said that he would sue Alvin.

After Bert had left, Alvin changed the price on the car to £25,000 and subsequently Cat came in and said she would like to buy the car, but that she would have to arrange finance.

On Tuesday Del came by and offered Alvin the full £25,000 cash there and then and Alvin sold it to him.

Required:

Identify whether there is a binding contract between:

(i)	**Bert and Alvin**	**(2 marks)**
(ii)	**Cat and Alvin**	**(2 marks)**
(iii)	**Del and Alvin.**	**(2 marks)**

(Total: 6 marks)

286 ARI (A) (PBE)

Ari operates a business as a designer of internet web pages for a variety of business clients. Unfortunately he has had some difficulty in recovering his full fees from a number of clients as follows:

(a) Bi, a newly qualified accountant, told Ari that although she could only raise the cash to pay half of the outstanding fees she would, as an alternative to paying the other half, do all of Ari's accountancy work for the coming year.

(b) Cas, a self-employed musician, told Ari that she could not pay any of the money she owed him. However, her father offered to pay Ari, but could only manage half of the total amount owed.

(c) Dex, a self-employed car mechanic, without contacting Ari, simply sent him a cheque for half of his fees stating that he could not pay any more and that the cheque was in full settlement of his outstanding debt.

Ari himself is now in financial difficulty and needs additional cash to maintain his business operation.

Required:

(a)	**Explain whether Ari can recover any of the money from Bi.**	**(2 marks)**
(b)	**Explain whether Ari can recover any of the money from Cas.**	**(2 marks)**
(c)	**Explain whether Ari can recover any of the money from Dex.**	**(2 marks)**

(Total: 6 marks)

287 BUD (A) (PBE)

Ali is a dealer in Persian rugs. As his business has been rather slow, he placed an advertisement in the Saturday edition of his local paper stating:

'Once in a lifetime opportunity to own a handmade Persian antique rug for only £1,500 – cash only. This is a serious offer – the rug will go to the first person who accepts it – offer valid for one day only – today Saturday.'

When Bud saw the advert, he immediately posted a letter of acceptance of Ali's offer in order to make sure he got the rug.

On Monday morning Bud's letter arrived, but by then Ali had changed his mind and decided he did not want to sell the rug.

Required:

(a)   Identify whether Ali's advertisement constitutes an offer or an invitation to treat.

(2 marks)

(b)   Explain whether there is a binding contract between Ali and Bud.   (4 marks)

(Total: 6 marks)

288 ABID (A) (CBE)

Abid regularly took his car to be serviced at his local garage, Bust Ltd. On the four previous occasions, before handing his car over to the garage, Abid had always been required to read and sign a contractual document which contained the following statement in bold red type:

'Bust Ltd accepts no responsibility for any consequential loss or injury sustained as a result of any work carried out by the company, whether as a result of negligence or otherwise.'

On the most recent occasion, due to the fact that the garage was very busy when he arrived, Abid was not asked to sign the usual document. He was, however, given a receipt for the car, which he accepted without reading. Bust Ltd's usual business terms were printed on the back of the receipt, including the statement above.

On driving the car home after its service, Abid was severely injured when the car suddenly burst into flames. It subsequently emerged that the fire had been the result of the negligent work by one of Bust Ltd's mechanics. Bust Ltd has accepted that its mechanic was negligent but denies any liability for Abid's injuries, relying on the exclusion clause above.

Task 1   (2 marks)

Which of the following TWO statements are correct?

- An exclusion clause can be incorporated into a contract by signature
- An exclusion clause can be incorporated into a contract by an implied term
- An exclusion clause can be incorporated into a contract by notice
- An exclusion clause cannot be incorporated into a contract by previous dealings

Task 2   (2 marks)

Which of the following statements is correct?

- An exclusion clause only needs to pass the common law rules
- An exclusion clause needs to pass the common law and statutory rules
- UCTA 1977 applies to consumer contracts
- CRA 2015 applies to consumer contracts

Task 3 (2 marks)

Which of the following TWO statements are correct?

- The exclusion clause has been incorporated through previous dealings
- The exclusion clause is void unless the courts consider it to be reasonable
- The exclusion clause is void as it attempt to exempt liability for personal injury
- The exclusion clause has not been incorporated

289 ANN (DEC 14) (PBE)

Ann owns a shop selling prints. She placed an advertisement in the Friday edition of her local paper stating:

'Unique opportunity to own a Bell print for £500 cash. Offer valid for one day only – tomorrow Saturday.'

When Con saw the advert, he immediately posted a letter of acceptance.

On Saturday, Di asked Ann if she would take a cheque for £500, but she refused to accept the cheque and told her she could not have the print. Later that day Ann sold the print to Evi.

On Monday morning Con's letter arrived.

Required:

In the context of the rules governing the creation of contracts:

(a)	Describe the precise legal nature of Ann's advertisement	(2 marks)
(b)	Explain whether Con has any right of action against Ann	(2 marks)
(c)	Explain whether Di has any right of action against Ann.	(2 marks)

(Total: 6 marks)

290 CROMWELL ARMS (CBE)

Oliver was selling his inn, the Cromwell Arms, and Charles was considering buying it. Charles wrote to Oliver's accountant, Richard, and requested information about the annual turnover of the inn. The accountant wrote to Charles informing him that the inn's annual sales were 'in the region of £200,000', adding that the information was given without any responsibility on his part.

Charles purchased the inn and subsequently found that although several years previously turnover had once approached £200,000, generally it was about £150,000 a year.

Task 1 (2 marks)

Which of the following TWO statements are correct?

- There is no need to show a loss has been made to make a claim for negligence
- There must have been a loss made to make a claim in negligence
- There must be a causal link to make a claim for negligence
- There is no need to show a causal link to make a claim for negligence

Task 2 (2 marks)

Which of the following loss is normally not recoverable?

- Loss as a result of personal injury
- Damage to property
- Financial loss directly connected to personal injury
- Pure financial loss

Task 3 (2 marks)

Which of the following TWO statements are correct?

- The accountant owes a duty of care to Charles
- The accountant does not owe a duty of care to Charles
- The accountant will be liable for the losses which Charles has suffered
- The accountant will not be liable for the losses which Charles has suffered

EMPLOYMENT LAW

291 FINE LTD (A) (CBE)

Fine Ltd specialises in providing software to the financial services industry. It has two offices, one in Edinburgh and the other, its main office, in London. In January 20X3 Gus was employed as a software designer attached to the Edinburgh office. However, by May 20X5, Gus was informed that he was to be transferred to the head office in London, which is more than 350 miles from his usual workplace.

Gus refused to accept the transfer on the basis that he had been employed to work in Edinburgh not London. Consequently, on 1 June 20X5 he wrote to Fine Ltd terminating his contract with them.

Task 1 (2 marks)

Which of the following TWO statements are correct?

- A claim for unfair dismissal is a common law action
- A claim for unfair dismissal is a statutory right
- A claim for unfair dismissal will be brought to an employment tribunal
- A claim for unfair dismissal must be brought to the County Court or High Court

Task 2 (2 marks)

Which of the following TWO statements regarding constructive dismissal are correct?

- It is where the employee breaches the contract
- It is where the employer breaches the contract
- The employee resigns as a result of the breach of contract
- The employee agrees to accept the termination of employment without payment in lieu of notice

Task 3 (2 marks)

Which of the following TWO statements are correct?

- Gus meets the minimum employment period requirement to make a claim for unfair dismissal
- Gus does not meet the minimum employment period requirement to make a claim for unfair dismissal
- The compulsory move would give rise to a claim for unfair dismissal
- The compulsory move would not give rise to a claim for unfair dismissal

292 EVE AND FRED (A) (PBE)

Dan operated a business providing statistical analysis in the financial services sector. Eve and Fred have both worked for Dan for three years. They were both described as self-employed and both paid tax as self-employed persons. Dan provided all of their specialist computer equipment and software. Eve was required to work solely on the projects Dan provided, and she had to attend Dan's premises every day from 9 am until 5 pm.

Fred, on the other hand, usually worked at home and was allowed to work on other projects. Fred could even arrange for his work for Dan to be done by someone else if he was too busy to do it personally.

As a result of the downturn in the financial services sector Dan has told Eve and Fred that there will be no more work for them and that they will not receive any further payment or compensation from him for their loss of work.

Required:

(a) Explain how courts use the economic reality (multiple) test to determine employment status. (2 marks)

(b) Identify whether:

(i) Eve would be classified as an employee or an independent contractor.
(2 marks)

(ii) Fred would be classified as an employee or an independent contractor.
(2 marks)

(Total: 6 marks)

THE FORMATION AND CONSTITUTION OF BUSINESS ORGANISATIONS

293 ELAINE (CBE)

Daniel is Elaine's friend. Elaine owns a toy business. One day whilst shopping for toys Daniel sees some goods which he thinks would be suitable for Elaine's business. He negotiates with Fred to buy some of these goods for himself and he thinks Elaine would be interested in buying some of Fred's goods too. Elaine is not answering her phone so Daniel cannot confirm with her that she authorises him to go ahead and buy the goods on her behalf.

Daniel goes ahead and makes the purchase on Elaine's behalf. When he purchases the goods he informs Fred he is purchasing them on Elaine's behalf.

Task 1 (2 marks)

With regards to an agency relationship which of the following statements is correct?

- The contract is made between the principal and the agent
- The contract is made between the principal and the third party
- The contract is made between the agent and the third party
- A binding contract cannot be created

Task 2 (2 marks)

Assuming Elaine agrees to buy the goods, which agency relationship has been established?

- Express agreement
- Implied agreement
- By ratification
- By estoppel

Task 3 (2 marks)

Which of the following TWO statements are correct in relation to ratification?

- Any contract can be ratified
- Elaine does not need to have been identified when Daniel made the purchase
- Elaine needs to ratify the whole contract
- Elaine must have the contractual capacity to make the contract

294 BLACK SHILLING (PBE)

Aarav instructs Joey to locate a specific rare coin called a 'Black Shilling.' For simply locating this coin, Joey will be paid £1,000, although no contract is drawn up. To aid in the search and to convince prospective sellers that Aarav is a serious coin-collector, Aarav gives Joey a 'White Shilling' from his collection to display to prospective sellers. Joey locates a seller, a contract is concluded and Aarav acquires the 'Black Shilling.'

Aarav has yet to pay Joey, but is requesting that his 'White Shilling' be returned.

Required:

(a) State the definition of an agent. (2 marks)

(b) Explain whether an agency relationship has been established between Aarav and Joey. (2 marks)

(c) Explain whether Joey has to return the 'White Shilling' in the absence of payment by Aarav. (2 marks)

(Total: 6 marks)

295 HAM, SAM AND TAM (A) (PBE)

Ham, Sam and Tam formed a partnership to run a petrol station. The partnership agreement expressly stated that the partnership business was to be limited exclusively to the sale of petrol.

In January 2008 Sam received £10,000 from the partnership's bank drawn on its overdraft facility. He told the bank that the money was to finance a short-term partnership debt but in fact he used the money to pay for a round the world cruise. In February Tam entered into a £15,000 contract on behalf of the partnership to buy some used cars, which he hoped to sell from the garage forecourt.

Required:

(a)   Explain the effect of an agency relationship within a partnership.   **(2 marks)**

(b)   Explain whether Sam has acted within his authority.   **(2 marks)**

(c)   Explain whether Tam has acted within this authority.   **(2 marks)**

(Total: 6 marks)

296 GEO, HO AND IO (A) (PBE)

Geo, Ho and Io formed a partnership three years ago to run a hairdressing business. They each provided capital to establish the business as follows:

Geo   £20,000

Ho   £12,000; and

Io   £8,000.

The partnership agreement stated that all profits and losses were to be divided in proportion to the capital contribution.

Unfortunately the business was not successful and the partners decided to dissolve the partnership rather than risk running up any more losses. At the time of the dissolution of the partnership its assets were worth £20,000 and its external debts were £7,000.

Required:

(a)   State TWO examples of when a partnership will automatically end without a court order.   **(2 marks)**

(b)   Explain how the assets will be distributed upon dissolution of the partnership.

(4 marks)

(Total: 6 marks)

297 DON (A) (PBE)

Don was instrumental in forming Eden plc, which was registered and received its trading certificate in December 2006. It has subsequently come to the attention of the board of directors that prior to the incorporation of the company Don entered into a contract in the company's name to buy computer equipment, which the board of directors do not wish to honour.

Required:

(a) State the legal effect of a pre-incorporation contract   **(2 marks)**

(b) Explain whether Eden plc is liable for the contract.   **(4 marks)**

(Total: 6 marks)

298 DOC (A) (CBE)

Doc, a supplier of building materials, entered into the following transactions:

An agreement to sell some goods to a longstanding friend, Ed. The contractual document, however, actually stated that the contract was made with Ed's company, Ed Ltd. Although the materials were delivered, they have not been paid for and Doc has learned that Ed Ltd has just gone into insolvent liquidation.

Doc had employed a salesman, Fitt, whose contract of employment contained a clause preventing him, Fitt, from approaching any of Doc's clients for a period of two years after he had left Doc's employment. Doc has found out that, on stopping working for him, Fitt has started working for a company, Gen Ltd, wholly owned by Fitt and is approaching contacts he had made while working for Doc.

Task 1   **(2 marks)**

Which of the following TWO are not considered to be a separate legal entity?

- **A sole trader**
- **A general partnership**
- **A limited liability partnership**
- **A public company**

Task 2   **(2 marks)**

Which of the following is NOT a consequence of Ed Ltd being a separate legal entity?

- **The shareholders of Ed Ltd are liable for the company's debts**
- **Ed Ltd can enter into contracts in its own name**
- **Ed Ltd owns property in its own name**
- **Ed Ltd has perpetual succession**

Task 3   **(2 marks)**

Which of the following TWO statements are correct?

- **Doc can take action against Ed personally**
- **Doc cannot take action against Ed personally**
- **Doc can enforce the restraint of trade clause against Fitt**
- **Doc cannot enforce the restraint of trade clause against Fitt**

299 GLAD LTD (DEC 14) (PBE)

Fred is a member of Glad Ltd, a small publishing company, holding 100 of its 500 shares. The other 400 shares are held by four other members.

It has recently become apparent that Fred has set up a rival business to Glad Ltd and the other members have decided that he should be expelled from the company. To that end they propose to alter the articles of association to include a new power to 'require any member to transfer their shares for fair value to the other members upon the passing of a resolution so to do'.

Required:

(a)   State the procedure which Glad Ltd must follow to alter its articles of association.

(2 marks)

(b)   Explain the effect of the requirement that any alteration to a company's articles of association must be for the benefit of the company as a whole.   (2 marks)

(c)   Explain whether or not the articles of association of Glad Ltd can be altered as proposed.   (2 marks)

(Total: 6 marks)

CAPITAL AND THE FINANCING OF COMPANIES

300 FAN PLC (A) (CBE)

Dee and Eff are major shareholders in, and the directors of, the public company, Fan plc. For the year ended 30 April 2009 Fan plc's financial statements showed a loss of £2,000 for the year.

For the year ended 30 April 2010 Fan plc made a profit of £3,000 and, due to a revaluation, the value of its land and buildings increased by £5,000.

As a consequence, Dee and Eff recommended, and the shareholders approved, the payment of £4,000 in dividends.

Task 1   (2 marks)

Which of the following TWO statements are correct?

• **Distributable profits is defined as accumulated realised profits less realised losses**

• **Distributable profits is defined as accumulated realised profits less accumulated realised losses**

• **A revaluation surplus is included within accumulated realised profits**

• **A revaluation surplus is not included within accumulated realised profits**

Task 2 (2 marks)

Identify which of the following documents would have been required to be submitted to Companies House when Fan Plc was registered?

	Required	Not required
Memorandum of association		
Application for registration		
Articles of association		
Statement of guarantee		

Task 3 (2 marks)

Which of the following TWO statements are correct?

- **The company could recover the distribution from Dee and Eff**
- **The company could not recover the distribution from Dee and Eff**
- **The company could recover the distribution from other shareholders**
- **The company could not recover the distribution from other shareholders**

301 JUDDER LTD (A) (PBE)

Hank is a director in Judder Ltd, which has an authorised and issued capital of 100,000 shares at a nominal value of £1. It has not traded profitably and has consistently lost capital for a number of years. Although the company has shown a profit on its current year's trading, its accounts still show a deficit of £50,000 between assets and liabilities. The board of directors thinks it would be beneficial if the company were to write off its previous losses and to that end are looking to reduce its share capital by £50,000.

Required:

(a) **State TWO statutory examples of why a company would reduce its share capital.**

(2 marks)

(b) **Explain the procedure involved in reducing Judder Ltd's share capital.** (4 marks)

(Total: 6 marks)

302 FIN (A) (PBE)

Two years ago Fin inherited £40,000 and decided to invest the money in company shares. He heard that Heave Ltd was badly in need of additional capital and that the directors had decided that the only way to raise the needed money was to offer fully paid up £1 shares to new members at a discount price of 50 pence per share. Fin thought the offer was too good to miss and he subscribed for 20,000 new shares. However, the additional capital raised in this way did not save the company and Heave Ltd has gone into insolvent liquidation, owing a considerable sum of money to its unsecured creditors.

Required:

(a) **State the meaning of the maintenance of capital principle.** (2 marks)

(b) **Explain Fin's potential liability for the debts of Heave Ltd.** (4 marks)

(Total: 6 marks)

303 INHERITANCE (A) (CBE)

Under the will of her late uncle, Clare has just inherited the following:

(a)   £10,000 of ordinary shares in A Ltd.

(b)   £5,000 of preference shares in B Ltd.

(c)   £5,000 debenture stock secured by a fixed charge against the assets of D plc

(d)   £5,000 debenture stock secured by a floating charge against the business and assets of E plc.

Task 1   **(2 marks)**

In relation to the above investment forms, which is the most secure?

- **Ordinary shares**
- **Preference shares**
- **Debenture stock secured by fixed charge**
- **Debenture stock secured by floating charge**

Task 2   **(2 marks)**

In relation to the above investment forms, which may have a cumulative right to dividends?

- **Ordinary shares**
- **Preference shares**
- **Debenture stock secured by fixed charge**
- **Debenture stock secured by floating charge**

Task 3   **(2 marks)**

In relation to the above investment forms, which normally participates in surplus capital?

- **Ordinary shares**
- **Preference shares**
- **Debenture stock secured by fixed charge**
- **Debenture stock secured by floating charge**

304 HO (DEC 14) (PBE)

Three years ago Ho subscribed for shares in two companies: Ice Ltd and Jet plc. In relation to the shares in Ice Ltd, Ho was only required to pay 50 pence per £1 share when he took the shares and was assured that he would not be required to make any further payment on them to Ice Ltd and the company passed a resolution to that effect. Unfortunately, Ice Ltd has gone into insolvent liquidation owing a substantial sum of money to its creditors.

In relation to the shares in Jet plc, Ho was required to pay a premium of 50 pence per £1 share. The shares are currently trading at 75 pence per share.

Required:

(a)   Describe any potential liability Ho may have with regard to the shares he holds in Ice Ltd and to whom any such liability would be owed.   **(2 marks)**

(b)   Explain the meaning and purposes of a share premium account.   **(2 marks)**

(c)   Explain whether Ho can gain access to the premium paid on the shares in Jet plc.
                                                                               (2 marks)

                                                                         (Total: 6 marks)

MANAGEMENT, ADMINISTRATION AND REGULATION OF COMPANIES

305 FRAN, GILL AND HARRY (A) (CBE)

In 2010 Fran, Gill and Harry formed a private limited company, Compuware Design Limited, to pursue the business of computer software design. They each took 100 shares in the company and each of them became a director in the new company. The articles of association of the company were drawn up to state that Fran, a qualified lawyer, was to act as the company's solicitor for a period of five years, at a salary of £10,000 per year.

In 2015 Gill and Harry found out that Fran had been working with a rival software company and has passed on some secret research results to that rival.

Task 1 (2 marks)

Which of the following TWO statements are correct?

- The articles of association are enforceable by the company against the members
- The articles of association are not enforceable by the members against the company
- The articles of association bind the company to members in any capacity
- The articles of association do not bind the company to members in any other capacity

Task 2 (2 marks)

Which of the following TWO statements are correct?

- Compuware Design Limited's articles of association can be altered by an ordinary resolution
- Compuware Design Limited's articles of association can be altered by a special resolution
- Fran can be removed from her position as a director by an ordinary resolution with special notice
- Fran can be removed from her position as a director by a special resolution with special notice

Task 3 (2 marks)

Which of the following TWO statements are correct?

- Fran cannot rely on the articles of association for her to remain as the company's solicitor
- Fran can rely on the articles of association for her to remain as the company's solicitor
- Gill and Harry cannot remove Fran from her role as company director
- Gill and Harry can remove Fran from her role as company director

306 KING LTD (A) (PBE)

King Ltd is a property development company. Although there are five members of its board of directors, the actual day-to-day running of the business is left to one of them, Lex, who simply reports back to the board on the business he has transacted. Lex refers to himself as the Managing Director of King Ltd, although he has never been officially appointed as such.

Six months ago, Lex entered into a contract on King Ltd's behalf with Nat to produce plans for the redevelopment of a particular site that it hoped to acquire. However, King Ltd did not acquire the site and due to its current precarious financial position, the board of directors have refused to pay Nat, claiming that Lex did not have the necessary authority to enter into the contract with him.

Required:

(a)   Explain a director's express authority.   **(2 marks)**

(b)   Explain whether Lex had the authority to enter into the contract with Nat. **(2 marks)**

(c)   Explain whether King Ltd is liable for the contract with Nat.   **(2 marks)**

(Total: 6 marks)

307 CLEAN LTD (A) (PBE)

Clean Ltd was established some five years ago to manufacture industrial solvents and cleaning solutions, and Des was appointed managing director.

The company's main contract was with Dank plc a large industrial conglomerate. The managing director of Dank plc is a friend of Des's and has told him that Dank plc will not be renewing its contract with Clean Ltd as he is not happy with its performance. He also told Des that he would be happy to continue to deal with him, if only he was not linked to Clean Ltd.

Following that discussion Des resigned from his position as managing director of Clean Ltd and set up his own company, Flush Ltd which later entered into a contract with Dank plc to replace Clean Ltd.

Required:

(a)   Explain any of his statutory duties as a director which Des has breached.   **(2 marks)**

(b)   Explain the remedies available to a company where a director has committed a breach of statutory duties and in particular what action can be taken against Des.

(4 marks)

(Total: 6 marks)

308 GOAL LTD (A) (PBE)

Goal Ltd is a property development company. Before its incorporation 12 months ago, its business was carried out by Hope, as a sole trader. On the formation of Goal Ltd, Hope expanded the business by asking three of his business contacts to supply additional capital in return for which they, together with Hope, became its directors. Although never formally appointed, Hope took the role and title of chief executive and the other directors left the day-to-day running of the business to him and were happy simply to receive feedback from him at board meetings.

Six months ago Hope entered into a contract, on Goal Ltd's behalf, with Ima to produce plans for the redevelopment of a particular site that it hoped to acquire. However, Goal Ltd did not acquire the site and due to its current precarious financial position and their fear of potential losses, the board of directors has refused to pay Ima, claiming that Hope did not have the necessary authority to enter into the contract with her.

Required:

(a) **Explain the implied authority of a Chief Executive.** **(2 marks)**

(b) **Explain whether Hope had the authority to enter into the contract with Ima and whether Goal Ltd is liable for the contract with Ima.** **(4 marks)**

(Total: 6 marks)

309 DO PLC (A) (CBE)

Chu, a suitably qualified person, was appointed as the company secretary of Do plc. Since his appointment, Chu has entered into the following contracts in the name of Do plc:

(a) an extremely expensive, long-term contract with Ex plc for the maintenance of Do plc's photocopiers

(b) an agreement to hire a car from Far plc which Chu used for his own, non-business related purposes

The directors of Do plc have only recently become aware of these contracts.

Task 1 **(2 marks)**

Which of the following TWO statements are correct?
* **Every company must have a qualified company secretary**
* **A public company must have a qualified company secretary**
* **The company secretary is usually appointed and removed by the members**
* **The company secretary is usually appointed and removed by the directors**

Task 2 **(2 marks)**

Which of the following TWO statements are correct?
* **Chu has express authority as stated in the articles of association**
* **Chu has express authority as delegated by the board**
* **Chu has implied authority regarding contracts of a commercial nature**
* **Chu has implied authority regarding contracts of an administrative nature**

Task 3 **(2 marks)**

Which of the following statements is correct?

- Both the agreements are binding on Do plc
- Neither of the agreements are binding on Do plc
- Only the contract for the maintenance of the photocopiers is binding on Do plc
- Only the contract to hire a car for personal use is binding on Do plc

310 KUT LTD (DEC 14) (PBE)

Kut Ltd is a small private company. Although there are three members of its board of directors, the actual day-to-day running of the business is left to Leo, who simply reports back to the board on the business he has carried out. Leo refers to himself as the chief executive officer of Kut Ltd, although he has never been officially appointed as such.

In October 2014, Leo entered into a normal business contract on Kut Ltd's behalf with Max. However, the other members of the board have subsequently lost confidence in Leo and have refused to pay Max, claiming that Leo did not have the necessary authority to enter into the contract with him.

Required:

(a) State the usual authority of individual directors to enter into binding contracts on behalf of their company. **(2 marks)**

(b) Explain whether or not Kut Ltd is liable to pay Max. **(4 marks)**

(Total: 6 marks)

INSOLVENCY

311 CRUMS LTD (A) (CBE)

At the start of 2006 Crums Ltd was faced with the need to raise a large amount of capital, which it was decided to raise through the mechanism of issuing a number of secured loans. In order to raise the capital Crums Ltd entered into the following transactions:

(i) it borrowed £50,000 from Don secured by a floating charge. The loan was given and the charge created on 1 February. The charge was registered on 15 February

(ii) it borrowed £50,000 from Else, also secured by a floating charge. This charge was created on the morning of 1 April and it was registered on 15 April

(iii) it borrowed £100,000 from Flash Bank plc. This loan was secured by a fixed charge. It was created in the afternoon of 1 April and was registered on 20 April

(iv) it borrowed £100,000 from High Bank plc. This loan was secured by a fixed charge. It was created on 5 April and was registered on 15 April.

Unfortunately the money borrowed was not sufficient to sustain Crums Ltd and in January 2007 proceedings were instituted to wind it up compulsorily. It is extremely unlikely that there will be sufficient assets to pay the debts owed to all of the secured creditors.

Task 1 (2 marks)

Which of the following statements are correct?

- A charge must be registered at Companies House within 14 days of creation
- A charge must be registered at Companies House within 21 days of creation
- A charge must be registered at Companies House within 28 days of creation
- A charge must be registered at Companies House within 30 days of creation

Task 2 (4 marks)

Identify the order of the debts in order of priority.

312 MAT, MARY AND NORM (A) (CBE)

On the advice of his accountant, Mat registered a private limited company to conduct his small manufacturing business in January 2010. One of the reasons for establishing the company was to avoid liability for potential losses. The initial shareholders of the company were Mat, his wife Mary, and her father Norm, who each took 1,000 shares in the company, each with a nominal value of £1. The accountant explained that they did not have to pay the full nominal value of the shares at once, so they each paid only 25 pence per share taken, with the result that they still owed the company a further 75 pence per share to be paid at a later date.

Unfortunately the business has not proved successful and Mat and Mary have decided that it is better to liquidate the company rather than run up any more debts. The current situation is that the company's land is worth £20,000 and it has a fixed charge of £20,000 secured against it. It has further assets to the value of £7,750, but it has debts to business creditors of £10,000 and owes the bank a further £10,000 on its bank overdraft. The liquidator's fee will be £2,000.

Task 1 (2 marks)

Which of the following TWO statements are correct?

- The shares can be treated as fully paid up
- The shares are treated as partly paid
- Mat, Mary and Norm are not required to contribute any further
- Mat, Mary and Norm will need to provide a further £750 each

Task 2 (2 marks)

The winding up will be a creditors' voluntary liquidation. Identify whether the following statements are true or false.

	True	False
A special resolution will be passed		
A declaration of solvency will be made		
A statement of affairs will be submitted		
A meeting of creditors must be held within 21 days		

Task 3 (2 marks)

Identify the order in which the debts will be repaid

	1st	2nd	3rd
Business creditors			
Bank overdraft			
Fixed charge			
Liquidator's expenses			

313 ADMINISTRATION (PBE)

Bouncy Time Ltd is a nationwide soft play hire company. The company leased additional new equipment and vehicles four months ago in order to meet an expected increase in demand. The total cost of leasing on a monthly basis amounts to £15,000 and there are further overhead and staff costs of £5,000. Unfortunately the level of demand expected has not materialised. Bouncy Time Ltd is generating about £10,000 a month in revenue.

The board of directors are concerned about the state of the business and are considering the possibility of putting the company into administration.

Required:

(a) Explain the purpose of administration. (2 marks)

(b) Explain the circumstances in which the court will agree to appoint an administrator. (2 marks)

(c) Explain whether an administration order to Bouncy Time Ltd would be granted. (2 marks)

(Total: 6 marks)

314 LIVERTON (PBE)

Liverton ltd is a private company that operates a long established and successful football club Liverton FC.

Due to poor performance by the football club in recent years the company has experienced falling revenues from ticket sales and merchandise. At the same time the company is incurring significant costs in players' wages and debt interest.

The board of directors are concerned that if the current financial situation continues, then the club will only be able to survive another 12 months. This is something the directors desperately wish to avoid, and are now considering all possible options to help them save the company.

Required:

(a) Explain why placing the company in administration might be a better alternative to liquidation. (4 marks)

(b) State two persons who can appoint an administrator. (2 marks)

(Total: 6 marks)

315 BRASSICK LTD (PBE)

Brassick Ltd has recently appointed an administrator to help secure its rescue from financial difficulties.

Despite the administrator now managing the day-to-day affairs of the company, the directors have continued to receive contact from various concerned parties.

(i) Saeed is a fixed charge creditor of the company, and is demanding that his loan is repaid or he will seize possession of the asset under charge.

(ii) Malcolm is a supplier who is owed £1,200. He handed a formal written demand for the amount due to one of the directors, and threatened to petition for a winding up of the company if the debt is not settled within 3 weeks.

(iii) Brian, a very unhappy shareholder, is threatening to gain support from other shareholders to force a winding up of the company.

The directors are unsure how these matters will affect the ongoing administration of the company.

Required:

(a) **Explain whether any of the above actions are likely to succeed whilst Brassick ltd is under administration.** (4 marks)

(b) **State the time period in which administration must normally be completed.**
(2 marks)

(Total: 6 marks)

316 WINSTON LTD (PBE)

The directors of Winston ltd have recently appointed an administrator to help rescue the company from its financial difficulties.

The directors are aware that a consequence of administration is that the powers of the board are suspended and the administrator assumes the day-to-day management of the company.

However, the directors are unsure whether they are legally required to make any parties aware of the appointment.

Required:

(a) **Explain the legal requirements regarding announcement and notification of the appointment of an administrator.** (4 marks)

(b) **Explain the time limit for the announcement and notification of the appointment of a liquidator.** (2 marks)

(Total: 6 marks)

317 MICHAEL (PBE)

Michael has approached you for advice in respect of the following companies in which he is a majority shareholder:

(i) Jordan plc was registered as a public company 11 months ago, however due to administrative problems within the company it has not yet obtained a trading certificate.

(ii) Cable ltd was registered as a private company 18 months ago, but for commercial reasons has never commenced business. The company will remain dormant for the foreseeable future.

Required:

(a) **For each of the above companies, explain whether there are grounds for compulsory liquidation by the court.** **(4 marks)**

(b) **State the persons that may petition the court for a compulsory liquidation.**

(2 marks)

(Total: 6 marks)

318 PAUL (PBE)

Paul is the sole shareholder of Hurst ltd, a private trading company.

Recently the company entered into financial difficulties, resulting in a number of suppliers being paid late, or in some instances not paid at all.

One of the company's suppliers Rex plc is owed £2,000. They served a formal written demand on Hurst ltd 6 weeks ago, but the amount still remains unpaid. Accordingly, in order to recover the amount due, the directors of Rex plc have been left with no option but to petition the court for a compulsory liquidation of Hurst Ltd.

Required:

(a) **State the grounds upon which Rex plc has petitioned for a winding up order.**

(2 marks)

(b) **Briefly explain the subsequent procedures involved in the compulsory liquidation of Hurst ltd.** **(4 marks)**

(Total: 6 marks)

319 SAMI LTD (PBE)

At the start of 2011, Sami ltd entered into the following transaction in an attempt to sustain its operation:

(a) It borrowed £200,000 from Martyn, secured by a floating charge. The floating charge was created on 1 May and it was registered on 12 May.

(b) It borrowed a further £250,000 from Glenn. This loan was secured by fixed charge created on 6 May and registered on 18 May.

(c) It borrowed £150,000 from a bank. This loan was secured by a fixed charge. It was created on 10 May and registered on 15 May.

Unfortunately this attempt to sustain its operation failed, and in September 2014 compulsory liquidation proceedings were begun. Initial estimates indicate it is highly unlikely that the company has sufficient assets to repay all of the above debts.

Required:

(a)   **Explain the order of repayment of the above debts.**   **(4 marks)**

(b)   **State who may register a charge and the time period for doing so.**   **(2 marks)**

(Total: 6 marks)

320   PARK LTD (PBE)

Park ltd is a private trading company registered in 2001. The company has enjoyed success through the years, but now the shareholders believe it is the right time to discontinue the operation, and bring the company to end.

The company has net assets of approximately £800,000, and its only liability is a secured bank loan of £50,000.

Required:

(a)   **State the procedures involved in a member's voluntary liquidation.**   **(4 marks)**

(b)   **State the circumstances in which a member's voluntary liquidation will convert into a creditor's voluntary liquidation.**   **(2 marks)**

(Total: 6 marks)

321   STRINE LTD (PBE)

Strine ltd is a private company manufacturing garden furniture. The company is financed by way of £200,000 of ordinary share capital, and a long-term bank loan of £800,000, which is secured by a fixed charge over the company's head office premises.

Since it began trading the company has always made modest profits. However in recent months they have experienced financial difficulties due to falling sales revenues and higher raw materials costs. As a consequence of this, the company has defaulted on its last 2 loan interest payments, and now the bank is very concerned about their ability to repay the outstanding loan.

On closer inspection of the company's accounts, the bank discovers that Strine ltd is insolvent, and they now intend to proceed with a creditor's voluntary liquidation.

Required:

(a)   **State the procedures involved in a creditor's voluntary liquidation.**   **(4 marks)**

(b)   **State two advantages of a floating charge to a borrower.**   **(2 marks)**

(Total: 6 marks)

CORPORATE FRAUDULENT AND CRIMINAL BEHAVIOUR

322 KEN (A) (PBE)

Ken is involved in illegal activity, from which he makes a considerable amount of money. In order to conceal his gain from the illegal activity, he bought a bookshop intending to pass off his illegally gained money as profits from the legitimate bookshop business. Ken employs Mel as his accountant to produce false business accounts for the bookshop business.

Required:

(a)   State the offence of money laundering.   **(2 marks)**

(a)   Explain whether Ken is liable for money laundering.   **(2 marks)**

(b)   Explain whether Mel is liable for money laundering   **(2 marks)**

                                                                       (Total: 6 marks)

323 SID AND VIC (A) (CBE)

Sid is a director of two listed public companies in which he has substantial shareholdings: Trend Plc and Umber Plc.

The annual reports of Trend Plc and Umber Plc have just been drawn up although not yet disclosed. They show that Trend Plc has made a surprisingly big loss and that Umber Plc has made an equally surprising big profit. On the basis of this information Sid sold his shares in Trend Plc and bought shares in Umber Plc. He also advised his brother, Vic, to buy shares in Umber Plc.

Task 1   **(2 marks)**

Which of the following TWO statements are correct?

- Sid is an insider because he receives the information from his position of a director
- Sid cannot be an insider as directors are excluded from the definition
- The information is not inside information as it will be made public within the next six months
- The information is inside information as it relates to particular securities, is specific and has not yet been made public

Task 2   **(2 marks)**

Which of the following TWO statements are correct?

- Sid is not guilty of an offence of insider dealing by selling his shares in Trend plc
- Sid is guilty of an offence of insider dealing by buying shares in Umber plc
- Sid is not guilty of an offence of insider dealing when he advises his brother to buy shares in Umber plc
- Sid is guilty of an offence of insider dealing when he advises his brother to buy shares in Umber plc

Task 3 (2 marks)

Which of the following TWO statements are correct?

- Vic has not committed an offence as he did not receive any specific information from Sid which encouraged him to buy the shares in Umber plc
- Vic has committed an offence as he has an indirect interest in Umber plc
- There are no defences to insider dealing
- It is a defence if it can be shown that there was no expectation of profit from the dealing

324 IRE LTD (A) (CBE)

Fran and Gram registered a private limited company Ire Ltd in January 2005 with a share capital of £300, which was equally divided between them, with each of them becoming a director of the company.

Although the company did manage to make a small profit in its first year of trading, it was never a great success and in its second year of trading it made a loss of £10,000.

At that time Fran said he thought the company should cease trading and be wound up. Gram however was insistent that the company would be profitable in the long-term so they agreed to carry on the business, with Fran taking less of a part in the day-to-day management of the business, although retaining his position as a company director.

In the course of the next three years Gram falsified Ire Ltd's accounts to disguise the fact that the company had continued to suffer losses, until it became obvious that they could no longer hide the company's debts and that it would have to go into insolvent liquidation, with debts of £100,000.

Task 1 (2 marks)

Which TWO of the following statements are correct?

- Fraudulent trading can only be a civil action
- Fraudulent trading can be a civil action and a criminal action
- Wrongful trading can only be a civil action
- Wrongful trading can be a civil action and a criminal action

Task 2 (2 marks)

Which TWO of the following statements are correct?

- Fraudulent trading applies only to directors and shadow directors
- Fraudulent trading must include dishonest intent
- Gram is liable for fraudulent trading
- Fran is liable for fraudulent trading

Task 3 (2 marks)

Which TWO of the following statements are correct?

- Gram is liable for wrongful trading
- Fran is liable for wrongful trading
- Wrongful trading applies only to directors and shadow directors
- Wrongful trading must include dishonest intent

325 BRIBERY (PBE)

Simran works for a science laboratory called Test-it Ltd. Her role is to test new products and issue health and safety certificates before the products are sold to the public. This is a rigorous procedure and can take several weeks if not months.

Simran has just received a call from Paula, the sales director of Angad plc, a company which manufactures food storage products. Paula explains that the company will be sending over a new product for testing but need to have the health and safety certificate by tomorrow so they can launch the product before one of their competitors. Paula knows that Simran enjoys wearing designer clothing and offers to send her a voucher for £2,000 which Simran can use to buy designer clothing at a well-known department store. Simran agrees to Paula's proposal.

Required:

(a) **Explain whether a criminal offence has been committed by Paula**   **(2 marks)**

(b) **Explain whether a criminal offence has been committed by Simran.**   **(2 marks)**

(c) **Explain whether a criminal offence has been committed by Test-it Ltd.**   **(2 marks)**

(Total: 6 marks)

326 NIT (DEC 14) (PBE)

Nit is involved in illegal activity, from which he makes a large amount of money. He also owns a legitimate taxi company and passes off his illegally gained money as profits of that business. Nit employs Owen, who is aware of the illegal source of the money, to act as the manager of the taxi company, and Pat as his accountant to produce false business accounts for the taxi business.

Required:

In the context of the law relating to money laundering:

(a) **Explain the meaning of layering.**   **(2 marks)**

(b) **Explain whether any criminal offences relating to money laundering may have been committed by Nit, Owen and Pat.**   **(4 marks)**

(Total: 6 marks)

Section 3

ANSWERS TO MULTIPLE CHOICE QUESTIONS

ESSENTIAL ELEMENTS OF THE LEGAL SYSTEM

1   B

Law created by Parliament is called statute.

2   C

The others are tracks of the civil courts.

3   C

4   B

Decisions of the Supreme Court are binding on the Court of Appeal.

5   C

6   A

The ratio decidendi is binding on lower courts.

7   B

8   A

9   C

The 1966 Practice Statement introduced this.

10   B

The stages are first reading, second reading, committee stage, report stage and third reading.

11   D

The balance of probabilities is what is required in civil cases.

12 A

This is as the Supreme Court is the only court higher than the Court of Appeal.

13 D

14 B

Civil law is a type of private law.

15 D

Where the material facts differ from a previous case the precedent does not need to be followed.

16 A

17 B

Criminal law is a type of public law.

18 B

In the event of conflict, equity will prevail.

19 A

The law created by judges through decisions in cases is known as case law.

20 D

This is where a body has acted ultra vires.

21 D

This is the final stage before a Bill becomes an Act.

22 A

Under the literal rule words are given their ordinary dictionary meaning.

23 C

24 C

25 B

26 A

27 C

28 A

29 C

THE LAW OF OBLIGATIONS

30 B

This was established in *Fisher v Bell*.

31 C

Silence cannot constitute acceptance.

32 B

This is the postal rule.

33 A

A warranty is an incidental term of the contract.

34 A

This was established in *Curtis v Chemical* Cleaning.

35 C

36 C

Damages contained in a penalty clause will not determine damages payable.

37 A

Damages are a common law remedy.

38 A

Breach of warranty can only result in a claim for damages.

39 C

These are essential elements of a contract.

40 A

41 A

42 B

43 **C**

44 **A**

45 **A**

46 **C**

A specialty contract will be required.

47 **A**

Revocation must be communicated but does not need to be in writing.

48 **B**

49 **C**

50 **A**

This was established in *Hyde v Wrench*.

51 **A**

Agreement constitutes offer and acceptance.

52 **C**

A counter-offer was made on the 5th April which brought the offer on the 1st April to an end.

53 **B**

In *Fisher v Bell* it was established that a window display is an invitation to treat.

54 **B**

55 **C**

56 **C**

This is not a factor in determining damages.

57 **B**

58 **C**

A breach of warranty only allows for damages as a remedy.

59   C

Consideration must have some monetary value even if it is insufficient.

60   B

The limitation period for contracts made by deed is 12 years.

61   C

62   A

63   A

64   D

65   A

Goods in a shop window are an invitation to treat, as established in *Fisher v Bell*.

66   C

Goods on display are invitations to treat, as established in the case of *Pharmaceutical Society of GB v Boots Cash Chemists*.

67   A

This was established in *Stevenson v McLean*.

68   A

An offer can be revoked at any time prior to acceptance as seen in *Routledge v Grant*.

69   A

Revocation can be communicated by a reliable third party as seen in *Dickinson v Dodds*.

70   D

Revocation only applies to offers.

71   B

72   C

The postal rule would seem to apply here, and therefore acceptance is deemed to be communicated when Stephen's letter is posted *(Adams v Lindsell)*, not when received by Martin.

73   C

Past consideration is not valid consideration, per *Re McArdle*. Consideration does not need to be adequate.

74   A

75   D

76   D

These are three ways in which a clause can be incorporated.

77   D

Bettini v Gye.

78   C

The courts presume that there is no intention to be legally bound in agreements between family members. The presumption is only ignored if there is clear evidence to the contrary.

79   C

80   B

Hochster v De La Tour.

81   A

The others are equitable remedies.

82   D

83   A

84   B

Loss of bargain damages would be awarded.

85   A

Past consideration has no value and is therefore not consideration. Therefore there is no agreement in place and Zoe does not have to pay for the services that Tabitha provided.

86   A

87   C & D

88   B

89 **A**

90 **C**

91 **A**

92 **A**

93 **A**

94 **B**

95 **B**

96 **A**

Damages will be reduced by a percentage determined by court.

97 **C**

This was established in *Caparo v Dickman plc*.

98 **D**

This is not one of the three tests which need to be satisfied.

99 **B**

The defendant's intent is not a relevant factor.

100 **A**

101 **A**

102 **C**

103 **C**

A higher level of care is owed to children.

104 **A**

This is the concept of special relationship.

105 **B**

106 **A**

107 D

108 B

109 B

110 B

111 D

112 C

113 A

EMPLOYMENT LAW

114 C

There is a duty to obey all lawful and reasonable orders.

115 B

Between 1 month – 2 years continuous employment there will be 1 week notice period.

116 C

This is an inadmissible reason.

117 C

118 B

119 B

120 C

121 C

122 A

The employer's intention is not a relevant factor.

123 B

This is not a necessary requirement.

124 B

This is an automatically unfair reason.

125 A

There is no implied duty to provide a reference.

126 C

127 B

This is not an automatically unfair reason.

128 C

Wrongful dismissal is a common law action.

129 C

130 B

Employees receive their pay net of all taxes and national insurance.

131 A

Pepper v Webb.

132 A

Redundancy pay is available after 2 years continuous employment.

133 C

134 B

135 A

136 C

Employment contract terms are also implied by statute. In common law employees have a duty to obey only lawful and reasonable orders.

137 D

138 D

139 C

Simmonds v Dowty Seals Ltd.

140   D

141   A

142   A

There is no legal duty on employers to provide a reference. If they choose to do so it must be honest and factual.

143   D

This is a common law duty.

144   A

145   C

146   C

147   A

148   A

149   B

150   B

THE FORMATION AND CONSTITUTION OF BUSINESS ORGANISATIONS

151   C

152   B

153   C

154   C

155   B

A statement of capital will be required.

156   B

157 **C**

158 **A**

Directors could be prosecuted for fraudulent trading.

159 **C**

160 **A**

161 **C**

Where an individual is personally liable for the business debts that person will be a sole trader.

162 **C**

163 **C**

164 **C**

165 **C**

There are no formal requirements to create an ordinary partnership.

166 **B**

The promoter will be liable under a pre-incorporation contract.

167 **D**

168 **A**

169 **C**

170 **A**

A partnership is not a separate legal entity, whereas a company is.

171 **D**

The articles of association are contractually binding on members and the company only in respect of membership matters.

172 **B**

A promoter is in a fiduciary position and should not make a secret profit.

173 **D**

174 C

175 A

Although the directors are bound by the articles, they are not bound to the company as such.

176 A

177 D

178 A

179 C

Foss v Harbottle.

180 D

181 B

Partnerships can only create fixed charges.

182 D

183 A

Public companies cannot be limited by guarantee.

184 D

185 D

186 C

187 D

Only private company names must end in Ltd.

188 B

Articles are not required to be submitted to form a company. Model articles will apply if no articles are submitted.

189 D

Allen v Gold Reefs of Africa.

190 A

191 B

192 D

193 D

194 C

195 A

CAPITAL AND THE FINANCING OF COMPANIES

196 A

197 A

198 B

199 C

200 B

201 B

202 B

203 C

204 A

205 C

206 A

207 B

208 C

209 D

210 C

211 B

212 D

The maximum expiry date is 5 years.

213 B

214 D

215 B

216 D

217 C

218 A

219 A

220 B

221 B

As Jabeen's charge was not registered within 21 days of creation, Adeel's charge takes priority.

222 B

Non-cash consideration must be received within five years.

223 C

224 D

MANAGEMENT, ADMINISTRATION AND REGULATION OF COMPANIES

225 C

226 C

227 A

228 A

229 C

230 C

231 A

232 A

233 C

234 C

235 C

236 A

237 D

238 B

Shadow directors have the same statutory duties.

239 A

Bushell v Faith.

240 A & D

241 A

242 B

243 D

Only offences committed in connection with the running or management of a company are grounds specifically set out in the Act.

244 C

245 D

246 D

247 A

It is only mandatory for public companies to have a company secretary.

248 B

249 A

INSOLVENCY LAW

250 C

251 C

252 A

253 C

254 B

255 A

256 C

257 B

258 A

The others would all rank as unsecured creditors.

259 A

260 D

A creditor owed £800 can only appoint an administrator upon application to the court. They cannot do so without court approval.

261 A

If an employee's contract is not adopted by the administrator within 14 days the employee is then made redundant.

262 C

263 A

264 A

265 A

266 B

267 C

CORPORATE FRAUDULENT AND CRIMINAL BEHAVIOUR

268 C

An action for civil liability can be brought if the company is being wound up. An action for criminal liability can be brought whether or not the company is in the course of being wound up.

269 B

270 B

271 C

272 A

273 B

274 A

275 D

276 D

277 D

278 B

An action for wrongful trading can only be brought where the company is in insolvent liquidation.

279 C

Section 4

ANSWERS TO MULTI-TASK QUESTIONS

THE LAW OF OBLIGATIONS

280 AMY AND BEN (A) (PBE)

(a) In domestic and social agreements, there is a presumption that the parties do not intend to create legal relations. The presumption may be rebutted by the actual facts and circumstances of a particular case (*Simpkins v Pays*).

(b) Although Amy and Ben are brother and sister it is clear from the facts of the situation that they entered into a business relationship with regard to the provision of the updating of the web site. In such circumstances there was a clear intention to create legal relationships and therefore Amy can enforce the contract against Ben.

281 ARTI (A) (PBE)

(a) Under the doctrine of anticipatory breach, one party prior to the actual due date of performance, demonstrates an intention not to perform their contractual obligations.

Express anticipatory breach occurs where a party actually states that they will not perform their contractual obligations (*Hochster v De La Tour*).

(b) The remedy of specific performance is not available in respect of contracts of employment or personal service. Therefore, Arti cannot be legally required to write the book for Bee Ltd.

(c) Bee Ltd can sue Arti for damages. Damages are intended to compensate an injured party for any financial loss sustained as a consequence of another party's breach.

282 AMY AND BRY (A) (PBE)

(a) The long established rule of contract was that the mere performance of a contractual duty already owed to the promisor could not be consideration for a new promise (*Stilk v Myrick*). Where, however, the promise did more than they were already contractually bound to do then the performance of the additional task does constitute valid consideration for a new promise.

The case of *Williams v Roffey Bros* expanded this to say that the performance of an existing contractual duty can amount to consideration for a new promise in circumstances where there is no question of fraud or duress, and where practical benefits accrue to the promisor.

(b)   In this situation Bry has clearly exerted a form of economic duress on Ami to force her to increase the contract price. Ami was left with no real choice but to agree to Bry's terms or else she would have suffered a potentially substantial loss. Such unfair pressure would take the case outside of *Williams v Roffey Bros* and Bry would be unable to enforce the promise for the additional £1,000.

283 BILD LTD (A) (CBE)

Task 1

- They compensate the injured party for any financial loss
- They put the parties in the position they would have been in had the contract been performed

Task 2

- It would be the difference in value between the building as it has been completed and its value if it had been properly completed
- It would be the cost of completing the work to the required specification unless the cost of remedying the defects are disproportionate to the difference in value between what was supplied and what was ordered

Task 3

- Damages of £2,000

284 ALI (A) (CBE)

Task 1

- An offer can be in any form
- An offer must be communicated to the offeree

Task 2

- The shop window sign and display is an invitation to treat
- Ben's letter to Ali is an offer

Task 3

- There is no contract between Ali and Ben
- There is a contract between Ali and Di

285 ALVIN (A) (PBE)

(a) (i)   The price notice on the car constituted an invitation to treat. As such it is not an offer to sell but merely an invitation to others to make offers (*Fisher v Bell*).

Consequently there is no contract between Bert and Alvin.

(ii) A promise to keep an offer open is only binding where there is a separate contract to that effect. This is known as an option contract, and the offeree must provide additional consideration for the promise to keep the offer open.

As Cat did not provide any consideration to form an option contract, Alvin is not bound to wait for her to return and can sell the car to anyone else if he so chooses.

(b) There is a perfectly ordinary contract between Del and Alvin where all the essential elements i.e. agreement and consideration are present.

286   ARI (A) (PBE)

(a)   As Ari agreed to accept Bi's offer to do his accounts as part payment of his outstanding debt there is nothing further he can do to recover any more money.

(b)   By accepting lesser payment from a third party, i.e. Cas's father, Ari cannot recover any more money from Cas.

(c)   Dex acted unilaterally and did nothing additional to compensate Ari for his part payment. Consequently Dex remains liable to pay Ari the remaining half of his bill (*D & C Builders v Rees and Re Selectmove Ltd*).

287   BUD (A) (PBE)

(a)   It might appear at first sight that Ali's advertisement in the paper was no more than an invitation to treat and therefore not capable of being accepted by any of the other parties. However, the wording of the advert was in such categorical terms that it might be seen to have been an offer to the whole world, stating his unreserved commitment to enter into a contract with the first person who accepted it.

(b)   Bud has clearly tried to accept the offer and would rely upon the postal rule of acceptance to press his case for getting either the rug or damages from Ali. His reliance on the postal rule would be to no avail, however, as the use of the post was clearly an inappropriate mode of acceptance. There was only one rug on offer: it was implicit in the advert that to get it, you had to turn up at Ali's showroom. Therefore Bud has not entered into a binding contract with Ali.

288   ABID (A) (CBE)

Task 1

- An exclusion clause can be incorporated into a contract by signature
- An exclusion clause can be incorporated into a contract by notice

Task 2

- An exclusion clause needs to pass the common law and statutory rules
- CRA 2015 applies to consumer contracts

Task 3

- The exclusion clause has been incorporated through previous dealings
- The exclusion clause is void as it attempts to exempt liability for personal injury

289   ANN (DEC 14) (PBE)

(a)   The first issue to determine is whether Ann's advertisement was an offer or an invitation to treat. An offer is a promise to be bound on particular terms. The offer may, through acceptance, result in a legally enforceable contract. Alternatively, an invitation to treat is an invitation to others to make offers. The person extending the invitation is not bound to accept any offers made to them. Usually, advertisements only amount to an invitation to treat and cannot be accepted to form a binding contract (*Partridge v Crittenden* (1968)). There are occasions, however, when an advert can amount to a genuine offer capable of acceptance by anyone to whom the offer is addressed (*Carlill v Carbolic Smoke Ball Co* (1893)). The wording of Ann's advert was in sufficiently categorical terms for it to have been an offer to the world at large, stating her unreserved commitment to enter into a contract with the first person who accepted it.

(b)   Once an offeree accepts the terms offered, a contract comes into effect and both parties are bound.

Usually, acceptance must be communicated to the offeror. However, there are exceptions, one of which arises where acceptance is through the postal service. In the latter circumstances, acceptance is complete as soon as the letter, properly addressed and stamped, is posted (*Adams v Lindsell* (1818)). The postal rule will only apply, however, where it is in the contemplation of the parties that the post will be used as the means of acceptance.

Con has clearly tried to accept the offer but his reliance on the postal rule would be to no avail as the use of the post was clearly an inappropriate mode of acceptance. He, therefore, has no right of action against Ann.

(c)   In order to form a binding agreement, acceptance must correspond with the terms of the offer. Thus the offeree must not seek to introduce new contractual terms into their acceptance (*Neale v Merritt* (1830)). Any attempt to do so amounts to a counter-offer and leaves the original offeror at liberty to accept or reject the new offer as they choose (*Hyde v Wrench* (1840)).

Ann's advertisement clearly stated that she wanted cash for the print and, therefore, Di's attempt to pay with a cheque did not comply with the original offer and leaves her with no grounds for complaint. The decision in *D & C Builders Ltd v Rees* (1966) as to cheques being equivalent to money is not to the point, as Ann wanted immediate payment for the print

Marking scheme		
		Marks
This question requires an explanation of the rules relating to the formation of contracts, especially the distinction between offers and invitations to treat and the rules of acceptance of offers.		
(a) 2 marks Good analysis and explanation of the nature of Ann's advertisement.		
1 mark Some explanation, but lacking in detail or application.		
0 marks No knowledge whatsoever of the topic.		
(b) 2 marks A good explanation of Con's situation in law.		
1 mark Some, but limited, explanation.		
0 marks No knowledge or explanation.		
(c) 2 marks A good explanation of Di's situation in law.		
1 mark Some, but limited, explanation.		
0 marks No knowledge or explanation.		
Total		6

290   CROMWELL ARMS (CBE)

Task 1

- There must have been a loss made to make a claim in negligence
- There must be a causal link to make a claim for negligence

Task 2

- Pure financial loss

Task 3

- The accountant owes a duty of care to Charles
- The accountant will be liable for the losses which Charles has suffered

EMPLOYMENT LAW

291   FINE LTD (A) (CBE)

Task 1
- A claim for unfair dismissal is a statutory right
- A claim for unfair dismissal will be brought to an employment tribunal

Task 2
- It is where the employer breaches the contract
- The employee resigns as a result of the breach of contract

Task 3
- Gus meets the minimum employment period requirement to make a claim for unfair dismissal
- The compulsory move would give rise to a claim for unfair dismissal

292   EVE AND FRED (A) (PBE)

(a)   Under the economic reality (multiple) test the court takes all the surrounding factors into account to determine an individual's status. The test involves asking whether the person who is doing the work, is doing so as a person in business on his own account.

(b)   (i)   Although the manner in which they Eve paid tax might indicate that she was self-employed, the fact that Dan provided her with equipment suggests that she was an employee. The most significant factor would appear the degree to which Dan controlled her. Eve had to work for Dan only and on his premises. This suggests clearly that although Eve was an employee.

(ii)   Fred was allowed to work for others but, most importantly, he was also allowed to use others to do his work for Dan. This suggests clearly that Fred was not employed by Dan.

THE FORMATION AND CONSTITUTION OF BUSINESS ORGANISATIONS

293   ELAINE (CBE)

Task 1
- The contract is made between the principal and the third party

Task 2
- By ratification

Task 3
- Elaine needs to ratify the whole contract
- Elaine must have the contractual capacity to make the contract

294 BLACK SHILLING (PBE)

(a) An agent is a person who is authorised to act for another, the principal, in the making of legal relations with third parties. An example would be where a director acts as an agent for his company.

(b) In this scenario there is an agency relationship by express agreement as Aarav has asked Joey to act on his behalf. An agency agreement can be made either orally or in writing.

(c) As an agent, Joey has the right to claim remuneration for the service he has performed which was agreed at £1,000. As Joey has not yet been paid he has the right to exercise a lien over the 'White Shilling' in his possession. A lien allows the agent to retain possession over the principal's property that is lawfully in the agent's possession until any debts due to the agent have been paid by the principal. Therefore, Joey can hold onto the 'White Shilling' until Aarav has paid him his remuneration.

295 HAM, SAM AND TAM (A) (PBE)

(a) S5 PA 1890 states that every partner is the agent of the firm and of the other partners. This means that each partner has the power to bind all partners to business transactions entered into within their express or implied authority.

(b) Sam has clearly used his powers for an unauthorised purpose. However, Sam has acted within his implied authority as a partner to enter into such a transaction. As a trading partnership, all the members have the implied authority to borrow money on the credit of the firm and the bank would be under no duty to investigate the purpose to which the loan was to be put.

(c) Tam's purchase of the used cars was clearly outside of the express provision of the partnership agreement. Nonetheless Tam would be likely to be held to be within the implied authority of a partner in a garage business (*Mercantile Credit v Garrod*).

296 GEO, HO AND IO (A) (PBE)

(a) Any of the following two:

   (i) The expiry of a fixed term or the completion of a specific enterprise

   (ii) One of the partners gives notice

   (iii) Death or bankruptcy of a partner

   (iv) Where continuation of the partnership would be illegal

(b) Firstly, the creditors will be paid their £7,000 in full from the £20,000 proceeds.

The remaining £13,000 will be distributed to the partners in proportion to their capital contribution.

Geo will receive £6,500 ($5/10 \times 13,000$)

Ho will receive £3,900 ($3/10 \times 13,000$)

Io will receive £2,600 ($2/10 \times 13000$)

297 DON (A) (PBE)

(a) A pre-incorporation contract is a contract which promoters enter into, naming the company as a party, prior to the date of the certificate of incorporation and hence prior to its existence as a separate legal person. The company cannot enter into a binding contract until it has become incorporated, and it is not bound by any contract made on its behalf prior to incorporation.

(b) The contract in the company's name was purportedly entered into before the company had come into existence. In such circumstances the company cannot be bound by the contract (*Kelner v Baxter*). Consequently, the provider of the computer equipment cannot take any action against Eden plc, but will have recourse to action against Don for any losses suffered by virtue of s.51 CA 2006.

298 DOC (A) (CBE)

Task 1

- A sole trader
- A general partnership

Task 2

- The shareholders of Ed Ltd are liable for the company's debts

Task 3

- Doc cannot take action against Ed personally
- Doc can enforce the restraint of trade clause against Fitt.

299 GLAD LTD (DEC 14) (PBE)

(a) Section 21 Companies Act 2006 provides for the alteration of articles of association by the passing of a special resolution, requiring a 75% vote in favour of the proposition. Consequently, the directors of Glad Ltd must call a general meeting of the company and put forward a resolution to alter the articles as proposed. Fred will be entitled to attend the meeting, speak and vote on the resolution.

If the resolution is successful, a copy of the new articles must be sent to the Companies Registry within 15 days.

(b) Any such alteration, as is proposed, has to be made 'bona fide in the interest of the company as a whole'. This test involves a subjective element, in that those deciding the alteration must actually believe they are acting in the interest of the company. There is additionally, however, an objective element requiring that any alteration has to be in the interest of the 'individual hypothetical member' (*Greenhalgh v Arderne Cinemas Ltd* (1951)). Whether any alteration meets this requirement depends on the facts of the particular case. In *Brown v British Abrasive Wheel Co Ltd* (1919), an alteration to a company's articles to allow the 98% majority to buy out the 2% minority shareholders was held to be invalid as not being in the interest of the company as a whole. However, in *Sidebottom v Kershaw Leese & Co* (1920), an alteration to the articles to give the directors the power to require any shareholder, who entered into competition with the company, to sell their shares to nominees of the directors at a fair price was held to be valid.

(c)   It is extremely likely that the alteration will be permitted. Fred only controls 20% of the voting power in the company and so he is no position to prevent the passing of the necessary special resolution to alter the articles as proposed. Additionally, it would clearly benefit the company as a whole, and the hypothetical individual shareholder, to prevent Fred from competing with the company, so Fred would lose any challenge he subsequently raised in court.

Marking scheme		
		Marks
This question requires an explanation of the rules relating to the alteration of a company's articles of association generally. It also requires an understanding of the way in which individual shareholders can have their right expropriated.		
(a)	2 marks Good analysis and explanation of the procedure for altering articles of association.	
	1 mark Some explanation, but lacking in detail or application.	
	0 marks No knowledge whatsoever of the topic.	
(b)	2 marks Good explanation of what is meant by in the interest of the company as a whole.	
	1 mark Some explanation, but lacking in detail or application.	
	0 marks No knowledge whatsoever of the topic.	
(c)	2 marks Good analysis of the likely outcome with reasons.	
	1 mark Some explanation, but lacking in detail or application.	
	0 marks No knowledge whatsoever of the topic.	
Total		6

CAPITAL AND THE FINANCING OF COMPANIES

300   FAN PLC (A) (CBE)

Task 1

* Distributable profits is defined as accumulated realised profits less accumulated realised losses
* A revaluation surplus is not included within accumulated realised profits

Task 2

	Required	Not required
Memorandum of association	✓	
Application for registration	✓	
Articles of association		✗
Statement of guarantee		✗

As the model articles will apply of no articles are supplied, it is not a requirement that articles must be sent, although all companies will have articles.

As Fan Plc is a public company it cannot be limited by guarantee and therefore a statement of guarantee would not be submitted.

Task 3

- The company could recover the distribution from Dee and Eff
- The company could recover the distribution from other shareholders

301 JUDDER LTD (A) (PBE)

(a)   Any two of the following examples:

Under s.621 Companies Act 2006 a company can reduce its capital for one of the following reasons:

(i)   To reduce or cancel liabilities on partly-paid shares.

(ii)   To return capital in excess of the company's needs.

(iii)   To cancel the paid-up capital that is no longer represented by the assets.

(b)   For private companies, such as Judder Ltd, a special resolution must be passed. This must be supported by a solvency statement made not more than 15 days before the date on which the resolution is passed.

A solvency statement is a statement made by each of the directors that the company will be able to meet its debts within the following year.

Copies of the resolution, solvency statement and a statement of capital must be filed with the Registrar within 15 days.

302 FIN (A) (PBE)

(a)   There are two key aspects of the doctrine of capital maintenance: firstly that creditors have a right to see that the capital is not dissipated unlawfully; and secondly that the members must not have the capital returned to them surreptitiously.

(b)   Shares cannot be issued at a discount to their nominal value. Therefore Fin will be liable to pay the balance of £10,000 and interest at the appropriate rate (s.580(2) CA 2006).

303 INHERITANCE (A) (CBE)

Task 1

- Debenture stock secured by fixed charge

Task 2

- Preference shares

Task 3

- Ordinary shares

304   HO (DEC 14) (PBE)

(a)   There is no requirement that companies should require their shareholders to immediately pay the full value of the shares. The proportion of the nominal value of the issued capital actually paid by the shareholder is called the paid up capital. It may be the full nominal value, in which case it fulfils the shareholder's responsibility to the company; or it can be a mere part payment, in which case the company has an outstanding claim against the shareholder. It is possible for a company to pass a resolution that it will not make a call on any unpaid capital. However, even in this situation, the unpaid element can be called upon if the company cannot pay its debts from existing assets in the event of its liquidation.

Applying this to Ho's case, it can be seen that he has a maximum potential liability in relation to his shares in Ice Ltd of 50 pence per share. The exact amount of his liability will depend on the extent of the company's debts but it will be fixed at a maximum of 50 pence per share.

(b)   It is common for successful companies to issue shares at a premium, the premium being the value received over and above the nominal value of the shares. Section 610 Companies Act 2006 provides that any such premium received must be placed into a share premium account. The premium obtained is regarded as equivalent to capital and, as such, there are limitations on how the fund can be used. Section 130 provides that the share premium account can be used for the following purposes:

(i)   to pay up bonus shares to be allotted as fully paid to members

(ii)   to write off preliminary expenses of the company

(iv)   to write off the expenses, commission or discount incurred in any issue of shares or debentures of the company

(v)   to pay for the premium payable on redemption of debentures.

(c)   Applying the rules relating to capital maintenance, it follows that the share premium account cannot be used for payments to the shareholders.

Applying the rules to Ho's situation, it can be seen that he cannot get any of the premium paid for the shares in Jet plc back from the company in the form of cash.

Ho would not even be able to recover the money indirectly as the shares are currently trading at below the nominal value, and at half of the premium price he paid.

Marking scheme			
			Marks
This question requires an explanation of the rules relating to shareholders' liability for shares.			
(a)	2 marks	Good analysis and explanation of the nature of Ho's potential liability.	
	1 mark	Some explanation, but lacking in detail or application.	
	0 marks	No knowledge whatsoever of the topic.	
(b)	2 marks	A good explanation of the share premium account and what it can be used for.	
	1 mark	Some, but limited, explanation.	
	0 marks	No knowledge or explanation.	
(c)	2 marks	A good explanation of Ho's inability to access the share premium account.	
	1 mark	Some, but limited, explanation.	
	0 marks	No knowledge or explanation.	
Total			**6**

MANAGEMENT, ADMINISTRATION AND REGULATION OF COMPANIES

305 FRAN, GILL AND HARRY (A) (CBE)

Task 1

- The articles of association are enforceable by the company against the members
- The articles of association do not bind the company to members in any other capacity

Task 2

- Compuware Design Limited's articles of association can be altered by a special resolution
- Fran can be removed from her position as a director by an ordinary resolution with special notice

Task 3

- Fran cannot rely on the articles of association for her to remain as the company's solicitor
- Gill and Harry can remove Fran from her role as company director

306 KING LTD (A) (PBE)

(a) A director is given express authority by the board of directors. Where authority is expressly given, all decisions taken are binding on the company.

(b) The board of King Ltd has permitted Lex to act as its Managing Director, and he has even used that title. The board has therefore acquiesced in his representation of himself as King Ltd's Managing Director and, consequently has the authority to enter into contracts within the scope of a Managing Director's implied authority.

(c) Entering into a contract to draw up plans would clearly come within the implied authority of a Managing Director. King Ltd will therefore be liable to pay Nat or face an action for breach of contract.

307 CLEAN LTD (A) (PBE)

(a) Des has beached his statutory duty under CA2006 s.175 by allowing a conflict of interest to arise without declaring it to the board and getting the approval of the other directors or indeed the members.

(b) The remedies available would include:

   (i)   Damages or compensation where the company has suffered loss

   (ii)   Restoration of the company's property

   (iii) An account of profits made by the director; and

   (iv)   Rescission of a contract where director failed to disclose an interest

   In this scenario, Des will be held liable to account to the company for any profits he made on the transaction.

308   GOAL LTD (A) (PBE)

(a)   Where there is no express authority, authority may be implied from the director's position. A chief executive will usually have authority to make commercial contracts on behalf of the company.

(b)   The board of Goal Ltd has permitted Hope to act as its chief executive, and he has even used that title. The board has therefore acquiesced in his representation of himself as Goal Ltd's chief executive and, consequently has the authority to enter into contracts within the scope of a chief executive's implied authority.

Entering into a contract to draw up plans would clearly come within the implied authority of a chief executive. Goal Ltd will therefore be liable to pay Ima or face an action for breach of contract.

309   DO PLC (A) (CBE)

Task 1

- A public company must have a qualified company secretary
- The company secretary is usually appointed and removed by the directors

Task 2

- Chu has express authority delegated by the board
- Chu has implied authority regarding contracts of an administrative nature

Task 3

- Both the agreements are binding on Do plc

310   KUT LTD (DEC 14) (PBE)

(a)   This question requires candidates to consider the authority of company directors to enter into binding contracts on behalf of their companies.

Article 3 of the model articles of association for private companies provides that the directors of a company may exercise all the powers of the company. It is important to note that this power is given to the board as a whole and not to individual directors and consequently individual directors cannot bind the company without their being authorised, in some way, so to do.

(b)   There are three ways in which the power of the board of directors may be extended to individual directors.

(i)   The individual director may be given express authority to enter into a particular transaction on the company's behalf. To this end, Article 5 allows for the delegation of the board's powers to one or more directors. Where such express delegation has been made, then the company is bound by any contract entered into by the person to whom the power was delegated.

(ii)   A second type of authority which may empower an individual director to bind his company is implied authority. In this situation, the person's authority flows from their position. The mere fact of appointment to a particular position will mean that the person so appointed will have the implied authority to bind the company to the same extent as people in that position usually do *Hely-Hutchinson v Brayhead Ltd* (1968)).

(iii)   The third way in which an individual director may possess the power to bind his company is through the operation of ostensible authority, which is alternatively described as apparent authority or agency by estoppel. This arises where an individual director has neither express nor implied authority. Nonetheless, the director is held out by the other members of the board of directors as having the authority to bind the company. If a third party acts on such a representation, then the company will be estopped from denying its truth (*Freeman and Lockyer v Buckhurst Park Properties (Mangal) Ltd* (1964)).

The situation in the problem is very similar to that in *Freeman and Lockyer v Buckhurst Park Properties (Mangal) Ltd*. The board of Kut Ltd has permitted Leo to act as its chief executive, and he has even used that title. The board has therefore acquiesced in his representation of himself as their chief executive and consequently Kut Ltd is bound by any contracts he might make within the scope of a chief executive's implied authority. As the contract in question is in the ordinary run of business, it would clearly come within that authority. Consequently Kut Ltd will be liable to pay Max or face an action for breach of contract.

Marking scheme		
		Marks
This question requires a consideration of the powers of individual directors to bind their company in contracts.		
(a)	2 marks Good explanation of the directors' powers collectively and individually.	
	1 mark Some explanation, but lacking in detail or application.	
	0 marks No knowledge whatsoever of the topic.	
(b)	3–4 marks A good explanation of express, implied and apparent authority plus appropriate application of that knowledge.	
	1–2 marks Some, but limited, explanation or application.	
	0 marks No knowledge or explanation.	
Total		6

INSOLVENCY

311   CRUMS LTD (A) (CBE)

Task 1

*   A charge must be registered at Companies House within 21 days of creation

Task 2

(i)   Flash Bank plc's loan, secured by a fixed charge created on 1 April.

(ii)   High Bank plc's loan, secured by a fixed charge created on 5 April.

(iii)   Don's loan, secured by a floating charge created on 1 February.

(iv)   Else's loan, secured by a floating charge created on the morning of 1 April.

312 MAT, MARY AND NORM (A) (CBE)

Task 1

- The shares are treated as partly paid
- Mat, Mary and Norm will need to provide a further £750 each

Task 2

	True	False
A special resolution will be passed	✓	
A declaration of solvency will be made		✗
A statement of affairs will be submitted	✓	
A meeting of creditors must be held within 21 days		✗

As the company is insolvent a declaration of solvency would not be made. A meeting of creditors must be held within 14 days.

Task 3

	1st	2nd	3rd
Business creditors			✓
Bank overdraft			✓
Fixed charge	✓		
Liquidator's expenses		✓	

The business creditors and bank overdraft would be grouped together as unsecured creditors.

313 ADMINISTRATION (PBE)

(a) Administration is often used as an alternative to putting a company into liquidation. The main aim is often to rescue a company in financial difficulty with the aim of allowing it to continue as a going concern. An administrator will be appointed to manage the affairs, business and property of a company.

(b) The courts will only agree to appoint an administrator if it is satisfied that the company is or is likely to become unable to pay its debts and that the administration order is likely to achieve its objectives.

(c) The issue facing Bouncy Time Ltd is whether the court will believe that the purpose of the order can be achieved. Bouncy Time Ltd has been running at a loss of £10,000 a month. In order to obtain an administration order it will have to be shown that this issue can be solved. If the company can argue that it is early days for the expansion and that it can make up the required shortfall in revenue then it has a reasonable chance of obtaining an administration order.

314   LIVERTON (PBE)

(a)   Liquidation is the process by which a company will completely cease to exist. Where companies are in financial difficulties with no prospect of recovery a liquidation may be the only course of action to take.

However an administration is often used as a means of rescuing a company in financial difficulty with the aim of allowing it to continue as a going concern. This is precisely what the directors of Liverton ltd want to achieve. Administration might also achieve a better overall outcome for creditors compared to a liquidation.

The process would involve the appointment of a licensed insolvency practitioner to act as administrator, who would then take over the management of the company's affairs from the directors. The administrator has wide powers to do things such as buy/sell assets, restructure debt, hire/dismiss employees etc. The hope is the administrator will take the necessary action to steer the company to financial safety.

(b)   Any of the following can appoint an administrator – choose any two:

(i)   The court in response to a petition by creditors

(ii)   A qualifying floating charge holder

(iii)   The directors of the company

315   BRASSICK LTD (PBE)

(a)   Appointing an administrator is predominantly a means of rescuing a company from financial difficulties i.e. the aim is that the company survives and continues to operate successfully. Accordingly the law provides certain protection in these instances to give the administrators the best chance of achieving this.

In this respect, the appointment of an administrator has the following important effects:

*   The rights of creditors to enforce any security over the company's assets are suspended until administration has ended. Therefore, Saeed will be unable to enforce his fixed charge.

*   Any petition for winding up the company is dismissed. Therefore, Malcolm will be unsuccessful in any petition for compulsory liquidation.

*   No resolution may be passed to wind up the company. Therefore, Brian and the other unhappy shareholders will be unable to pursue a winding up.

(b)   Administration must normally be completed within 12 months of commencement. However this may be extended at the consent of the court or the company's secured creditors.

316 WINSTON LTD (PBE)

(a) Legal requirements relating to announcement and appointment of an administrator include:

- The administrator must publish a notice of appointment in the London Gazette and in a newspaper in the area where Winston Ltd has its principal place of business.

- They must obtain a full list of Winton Ltd's creditors and send notice of appointment to each of them.

- They must send of notice of appointment to the registrar.

- They must ensure that every business document bears their identity as administrator, and that he/she is managing the affairs, business and property of the company.

(b) Generally notification of appointment must be made as soon as is reasonably practicable after appointment, however specifically the registrar must be informed within 7 days of appointment.

317 MICHAEL (PBE)

(a) The possible grounds for a compulsory liquidation are set out in s.122 Insolvency Act 1986. Applying these to the companies in the question:

Jordan plc – s.122(1)(b) provides that where a public company has not been issued with a trading certificate within 12 months of incorporation, there are grounds for a compulsory winding up by the court. The company therefore has 1 month to obtain a trading certificate before this action can be taken.

Cable ltd – s.122(1)(d) provides that where a company has not commenced business within a year of being incorporated, this is grounds for a compulsory winding up by the court. This would appear to apply in this instance.

In all instances, companies may pass a special resolution to be wound up by the court under s.122(1)(a), although this is rare.

(b) Under s.124 the following persons may petition the court for a compulsory liquidation.

(i) The company itself

(ii) The official receiver

(iii) The Department for Business, Enterprise and Regulatory Reform

(iv) A contributory

(v) A creditor who is owed at least £750

318 PAUL (PBE)

(a) S.122(1)(f) The company is unable to pay its debts.

S.123 A company is deemed unable to pay its debts where a creditor who is owed at least £750 has served a written demand for payments and the company has failed to pay the sum due within three weeks

(b) The procedures set out in the Insolvency Act 1986 are as follows:

(i) On the making of the winding up order, the official receiver becomes liquidator of Hurst ltd.

(ii) Within 12 weeks, the official receiver will summon meetings of the creditors and contributories in order to appoint a licensed insolvency practitioner to take over the job of liquidator and to appoint a liquidation committee.

(iii) The liquidator is responsible for realising the assets and distributing the proceeds.

(iv) The liquidator presents his report to final meetings of the members and creditors.

(v) The liquidator informs the registrar of the final meeting and submits a copy of their report.

(vi) The registrar registers the report and the company is dissolved 3 months later.

319 SAMI LTD (PBE)

(a) The correct order or repayment is as follows:

(i) Glenn's loan secured by a fixed charge created on 6 May

(ii) Bank loan secured by a fixed charge created on 10 May

(iii) Martyn's Loan secured by floating charge created on 1 May

Fixed charges are repaid in priority to floating charges. Where there is more than one fixed charge holder, priority follows the order in which they were created.

In the case of Sami ltd, Glenn's loan was created first and therefore receives priority over the bank loan, regardless of the fact that the charge on the bank loan was registered before Glenn's.

Floating charge holders rank behind fixed charge holders, the liquidator, and preferential creditors. Accordingly Martyn stands at most risk of not receiving the full amount of his loan back on the liquidation.

(b) Charges can be registered by the company or the charge holder.

Charges must be registered within 21 days of creation.

320 PARK LTD (PBE)

(a) The Insolvency Act 1986 sets out the following procedures for a member's voluntary liquidation:

(i) Winding up commences on the passing of a special resolution by members of Park ltd

(ii) The directors of the company must make a declaration of solvency, which declares the company will be able to fully repay all its debts within the next 12 months.

(iii) The members of Park ltd will then appoint a licensed insolvency practitioner as liquidator.

(iv) The liquidator will operate to realise the assets of the company and distribute the proceeds according to specific rules of priority.

(v) The liquidator presents their report to a final meeting of members.

(vi) Finally the liquidator informs the registrar of companies, and the company is dissolved 3 months later.

(b) A member's liquidation converts to a creditor's liquidation where it becomes clear to the liquidator that the company is unable to repay its debts in accordance with the declaration of solvency.

In simple terms, this is seen where a company initially considered itself to be in a solvent position, but later it is discovered that in fact it is insolvent.

321 STRINE LTD (PBE)

(a) The Insolvency Act 1986 sets out the following procedures for a member's voluntary liquidation:

(i) Winding up commences on the passing of a special resolution by members of Strine ltd

(ii) A meeting of creditors is held within 14 days of the resolution being passed.

(iii) The directors of Strine ltd must submit a statement of company's affairs.

(iv) A licensed insolvency practitioner is appointed to undertake the realisation of company assets, and distribution of proceeds. The appointment is made by with the members or the creditors, although the creditors' choice will prevail in the event of dispute.

(v) A liquidation committee is appointed by members and creditors to oversee the work of the liquidator.

(vi) The liquidator presents their report in a final meeting of members and creditors, before informing the registrar of companies.

(b) The borrowing company can deal freely with the assets under charge.

There is flexibility for the borrower because a wider class of assets can be charged, such as stock and debtors.

CORPORATE FRAUDULENT AND CRIMINAL BEHAVIOUR

322 KEN (A) (PBE)

(a) Money laundering is the process by which the proceeds of crime are converted into assets which appear to have a legal rather than an illegal source. The aim of disguising the source of the property is to allow the holder to enjoy it free from suspicion as to its source.

(b) If the original money to purchase the bookshop was the product if crime, then that transaction itself was an instance of money laundering. However, even if that was not the case and the bookshop was bought with legitimate money, it is nonetheless the case that it is being used to conceal the fact that the source of much of Ken's money is criminal activity. Ken would therefore be guilty on the primary offence of money laundering under the Proceeds of Crime Act 2002.

(c) Mel is guilty of an offence as she is assisting Ken in his money laundering procedure by producing false accounts. Her activity is covered by the offence of actively concealing and disguising criminal property.

323 SID AND VIC (A) (CBE)

Task 1

- Sid is an insider because he receives the information from his position of a director
- The information is inside information as it relates to particular securities, is specific and has not yet been made public

Task 2

- Sid is guilty of an offence of insider dealing by buying shares in Umber plc
- Sid is guilty of an offence of insider dealing when he advises his brother to buy shares in Umber plc

Task 3

- Vic has not committed an offence as he did not receive any specific information from Sid which encouraged him to buy the shares in Umber plc
- It is a defence if it can be shown that there was no expectation of profit from the dealing

324 IRE LTD (A) (CBE)

Task 1

- Fraudulent trading can be a civil action and a criminal action
- Wrongful trading can only be a civil action

Task 2

- Fraudulent trading must include dishonest intent
- Gram is liable for fraudulent trading

Task 3

- Fran is liable for wrongful trading
- Wrongful trading applies only to directors and shadow directors

325 BRIBERY (PBE)

(a) Paula is guilty of bribery under s.1 of the Act as she is bribing Simran by offering her a voucher in return for her issuing a health and safety certificate without following the appropriate procedures.

(b) When Simran accepts the voucher and issues the certificate she will be guilty of receiving a bribe from Paula under s.2 of the Act.

(c) Test-it Ltd could be guilty of bribery under s.7 of the Act for failing to prevent bribery unless they can show under s.9 that they had in place 'adequate procedures'.

326 NIT (DEC 14) (PBE)

(a) Money laundering is a criminal offence under the Proceeds of Crime Act (POCA) 2002. Layering is one of the stages in the overall process of money laundering designed to disguise the illegal source of money. It involves the transfer of money made from illegal sources from place to place and from one business to another in order to conceal the initial illegal source of the money. The layering process may involve many inter-business transfers in an attempt to confuse any potential investigation of the original source of the money.

(b) The POCA 2002 seeks to control money laundering by creating three categories of criminal offences in relation to that activity.

- **laundering**

  The principal money laundering offence relates to laundering the proceeds of crime or assisting in that process. Under s.327, it is an offence to conceal, disguise, convert, transfer or remove criminal property.

- **failure to report**

  The second category of offence relates to failing to report a knowledge or suspicion of money laundering. Under s.330 POCA 2002 it is an offence for a person who knows or suspects that another person is engaged in money laundering not to report the fact to the appropriate authority.

- **tipping off**

  The third category of offence relates to tipping off. Section 333 POCA 2002 makes it an offence to make a disclosure, which is likely to prejudice any investigation under the Act.

It is apparent from the scenario that all three people involved in the scenario are liable to prosecution under the POCA 2002 as they are involved in money laundering. If the original money to establish the taxi company was the product of crime, then that transaction itself was an instance of money laundering. However, even if that were not the case and the taxi company had been bought from legitimate money, it is nonetheless the case that it is being used to conceal the fact that the source of much of Nit's money is criminal activity.

Nit would therefore be guilty on the primary offence of money laundering under s.327 POCA 2002.

Whether or not Owen is also guilty of an offence in relation to the POCA depends on the extent of his knowledge as to what is actually going on in the company. As he knows what is taking place, then, as he is clearly assisting Nit in his money laundering procedure, his activity is covered by s.327, as he is actively concealing and disguising criminal property. He would also be liable under s.328 as his arrangement with Nit 'facilitates the retention of criminal property'.

Pat is also guilty under the same provisions as Owen, in that he is actively engaged in the money laundering process, by producing false accounts. Had he not been an active party to the process, he might nonetheless have been liable, under s.330, for failing to disclose any suspiciously high profits from the taxi business.

Marking scheme	
	Marks
This question requires a consideration of the law relating to money laundering.	
(a) 2 marks Good explanation of the process of layering in the context of money laundering.	
1 mark Some explanation, but lacking in detail or application.	
0 marks No knowledge whatsoever of the topic.	
(b) 3–4 marks A good explanation of the potential crimes under the Proceeds of Crime Act 2002 plus appropriate application of that knowledge.	
1–2 marks Some, but limited, explanation or application.	
0 marks No knowledge or explanation.	
Total	6

Fundamentals Level – Skills Module

Corporate and Business Law (English)

Specimen Exam applicable from
December 2014

Time allowed: 2 hours

This paper is divided into two sections:

Section A – ALL 45 questions are compulsory and MUST be
attempted

Section B – ALL FIVE questions are compulsory and MUST be
attempted

Do NOT open this paper until instructed by the supervisor.

**You must NOT write in your answer booklet until instructed by the
supervisor.**

This question paper must not be removed from the examination hall.

The Association of Chartered Certified Accountants

Section A – ALL 45 questions are compulsory and MUST be attempted

Please use the space provided on the inside cover of the Candidate Answer Booklet to indicate your chosen answer to each multiple choice question.

1   Which of the following may imply terms into contracts?

    A   Statute
    B   Third parties
    C   The parties to the contract

                           (1 mark)

2   There are a number of ways in which investors can take an interest in a company and such different interests have different rights attached to them.

    Which of the following NORMALLY participate in surplus capital?

    A   Preference shares
    B   Ordinary shares
    C   Debentures secured by a fixed charge
    D   Debentures secured by a floating charge

                           (2 marks)

3   In the context of the English legal system, which of the following courts ONLY has civil jurisdiction?

    A   Magistrates' court
    B   County court
    C   High Court

                           (1 mark)

4   In the context of employment law, which of the following is an AUTOMATICALLY fair ground for dismissing an employee?

    A   Unofficial industrial action
    B   Redundancy
    C   Refusal to join a trade union
    D   Legal prohibition

                           (2 marks)

5   Which of the following business forms does the use of the abbreviation 'Ltd' after the name of a business indicate?

    A   A limited partnership
    B   A limited liability partnership
    C   A private limited company

                           (1 mark)

6 Jas has been continuously employed for six years.

Which of the following states the minimum period of notice she is entitled to?

A One month
B Six weeks
C Three months

(1 mark)

7 **Which of the following is indicated by the abbreviation 'Ltd' at the end of a company's name?**

A The shares are not transferable
B The shares may not be offered to the public
C The shares are freely transferable on the stock exchange

(1 mark)

8 Section 122 Insolvency Act 1986 specifically provides a distinct ground for applying to have a company wound up on the ground that it is just and equitable to do so.

Which of the following parties may petition to have a company compulsorily wound up under that provision?

A Shareholders of the company
B Creditors of the company
C Debentureholders of the company
D The Secretary of State

(2 marks)

9 Mo has a significant holding in the shares of Nova Ltd. He wishes to use his shareholding to remove Owen from the board of directors but is not sure how to do so.

Which of the following must be used to remove a director from office?

A An ordinary resolution
B An ordinary resolution with special notice
C A special resolution
D A written resolution

(2 marks)

10 A written ordinary resolution requires the approval of which of the following?

A More than 50% of those actually voting
B More than 50% of those entitled to vote
C Unanimous approval of those entitled to vote

(1 mark)

[P.T.O.

11 Employment law is a mixture of common law and statutory provisions.

Which of the following is purely based on statute law?

A Summary dismissal
B Unfair dismissal
C Wrongful dismissal

(1 mark)

12 Jo's contract of employment states that she is employed in Glasgow. When her employer tells her that she has to work in London, some 500 miles away, Jo immediately resigns.

Which of the following may this be considered an example of?

A Unfair dismissal
B Constructive dismissal
C Summary dismissal

(1 mark)

13 **Which parties are bound by the terms of the tender when one party submits a tender?**

A The person submitting the tender
B The person requesting the tender
C Both parties
D Neither party

(2 marks)

14 **In the context of contract law, a bid at an auction is which of the following?**

A An invitation to treat
B An offer
C A counter-offer
D An acceptance

(2 marks)

15 Bee injured her eye after failing to close a safety gate on a machine as instructed. She was also not wearing mandatory safety goggles as required by her contract of employment.

Which of the following is this an example of?

A Novus actus interveniens
B Volenti non fit injuria
C Res ipsa loquitur
D Contributory negligence

(2 marks)

16 What is the effect of a finding of contributory negligence in the law of tort?

    A   It removes the requirement to pay damages
    B   It reverses the payment of damages
    C   It decreases the level of damages

(1 mark)

17 In the context of the English legal system, which of the following courts ONLY has criminal jurisdiction?

    A   Magistrates' court
    B   Crown Court
    C   County court

(1 mark)

18 Imran claims that Zak owes him £1,000 as a result of a breach of contract.

In which court will Imran start his action against Zak?

    A   The magistrates' court
    B   The county court
    C   The High Court

(1 mark)

19 In the context of case law, which of the following applies to an *obiter dictum*?

    A   It is binding on all future courts
    B   It is binding on all lower courts
    C   It is not binding on any courts
    D   It is not binding outside the court it was issued in

(2 marks)

20 Contributory negligence arises as a result of the fault of which of the following?

    A   The claimant
    B   The respondent
    C   A third party

(1 mark)

21 Ann got trapped in a public toilet due to the lock being faulty. Rather than wait for help, she tried to climb out of the window but fell and broke her leg.

Which of the following is this an example of?

    A   Res ipsa loquitur
    B   Volenti non fit injuria
    C   Novus actus interveniens
    D   Contributory negligence

(2 marks)

[P.T.O.

22 The law treats employees differently from the self-employed and has established a number of tests to distinguish between the two categories.

Which of the following is NOT a test for establishing an employment relationship?

A   The subordinate test
B   The control test
C   The integration test
D   The economic reality test

(2 marks)

23 Breach of which of the following terms does NOT allow the possibility of the aggrieved party terminating the contract?

A   A condition
B   A warranty
C   An innominate term

(1 mark)

24 Which of the following, in the context of entering into a contract, constitutes a binding offer to sell a unique item of furniture?

A   Placing an advert in a newspaper with a price attached
B   Placing it on display inside a shop with a price attached
C   Telling someone the price you may be willing to accept for it
D   Telling someone you will reduce the marked price on it by 10%

(2 marks)

25 Mark has received the agenda for the annual general meeting of Rova Ltd, a company he has shares in. The agenda contains a number of resolutions to be proposed at the meeting, but being a new member Mark is not certain as to what is exactly involved.

In the context of company meetings, which of the following must be passed by a 75% majority to be effective?

A   An ordinary resolution with special notice
B   A special resolution
C   A written resolution

(1 mark)

26 Section 122 Insolvency Act 1986 provides a number of distinct grounds for applying to have a company wound up on a compulsory basis.

Which of the following is NOT a ground for the compulsory winding up of a company under that provision?

A   The company has not received a trading certificate within its first 12 months
B   The company has not started trading within the first 12 months
C   The company has suspended its business for 12 months
D   The company has altered its primary business within the first 12 months

(2 marks)

27 Abe issued an invitation to tender for a contract and Bea submitted her terms.

Which of the following statements is accurate?

   A   Abe made an offer which Bea accepted
   B   Abe made an invitation to treat and Bea made an offer
   C   Both Abe and Bea made invitations to treat
   D   Abe made an offer and Bea made a counter-offer

(2 marks)

28 **In the context of statutory interpretation, which of the following requires judges to consider the wrong which the legislation was intended to prevent?**

   A   The mischief rule
   B   The literal rule
   C   The golden rule

(1 mark)

29 It is not unusual for some company investments to carry cumulative dividend rights.

Which of the following statements about the declaration of cumulative dividends is correct?

   A   They are not paid until profits reach a certain percentage
   B   They are paid in the form of a bonus issue
   C   They are paid out of capital
   D   They are paid when profits are available for that purpose

(2 marks)

30 **Which of the following statements in relation to effective consideration is correct?**

   A   It must be both adequate and sufficient
   B   It must be adequate but need not be sufficient
   C   It must be sufficient but need not be adequate

(1 mark)

31 **In the context of the English legal system, which of the following defines the *ratio decidendi* of a judgement?**

   A   The decision in a previous case
   B   The facts of the case
   C   The legal reason for deciding the case
   D   The future application of the case

(2 marks)

32 Dan has been accused of a criminal offence and is due to be tried soon. He denies responsibility, claiming that the prosecution has no evidence that he committed the offence in question.

Which of the following describes the standard of proof in a criminal case?

A   On the balance of probability
B   On the balance of certainty
C   Beyond reasonable doubt
D   Beyond evident doubt

(2 marks)

33 **Which of the following statements relating to limited liability partnerships is correct?**

A   They are limited to a maximum of 20 members
B   They must have a minimum of two members
C   They must have at least one unlimited member

(1 mark)

34 Ho subscribed for some partly paid-up shares in Io Ltd. The company has not been successful and Ho has been told that when Io Ltd is liquidated, he will have to pay the amount remaining unpaid on his shares. However, he is not sure to whom such payment should be made.

In limited liability companies, shareholders are liable to which party for any unpaid capital?

A   Creditors
B   The directors
C   The company
D   The liquidator

(2 marks)

35 **Which of the following CANNOT petition for the compulsory winding up of a company on the grounds of INSOLVENCY under s.122 Insolvency Act 1986?**

A   The board of directors
B   The members of the company
C   The company's creditors
D   The Secretary of State

(2 marks)

36 Money laundering involves a number of phases in the overall procedure.

Which TWO of the following are recognised phases in money laundering?

(1) Relocation
(2) Layering
(3) Integration
(4) Distribution

A   1 and 2
B   1 and 4
C   2 and 3
D   3 and 4

(2 marks)

37 **Which TWO of the following are AUTOMATICALLY unfair grounds for dismissing an employee?**

(1) Engaging in trade union activity
(2) Constructive dismissal
(3) Dismissal on transfer of employment to a new undertaking
(4) Redundancy

A   1 and 2
B   2 and 3
C   3 and 4
D   1 and 3

(2 marks)

38 **In the context of the law of agency, an agent will NOT be liable for a contract in which of the following instances?**

A   Where the agent fails to disclose that they are acting as such
B   Where the agent intends to take the benefit of the contract and does not disclose they are acting as an agent
C   Where the agent acts on their own behalf although claiming to be an agent

(1 mark)

39 The Employment Rights Act (ERA) 1996 sets out remedies in relation to unfair dismissal.

Which of the following is NOT a potential remedy for unfair dismissal under the ERA 1996?

A   Reinstatement
B   Re-engagement
C   Re-employment

(1 mark)

[P.T.O.

40 Which TWO statements are correct in relation to designated members in limited liability partnerships (LLPs)?

(1) They must not take part in the day-to-day operation of the business
(2) They are responsible for filing the LLP's accounts
(3) They are fully liable for partnership debts
(4) They have limited liability

A 1 and 4
B 2 and 4
C 2 and 3
D 1 and 3

(2 marks)

41 The term insider dealing relates to a number of potential criminal offences.

Which TWO of the following are crimes in relation to insider dealing?

(1) Encouraging someone to engage in insider dealing
(2) Failing to report insider dealing
(3) Concealing insider dealing
(4) Passing on inside information

A 1 and 2
B 1 and 4
C 2 and 3
D 2 and 4

(2 marks)

42 **Which of the following can be accepted so as to form a binding contract?**

A A supply of information
B A statement of intent
C A quotation of price
D An agreement to enter into a future contract

(2 marks)

43 Contracts are legally enforceable agreements.

Which of the following statements regarding contractual agreements is true?

A They must be in writing
B They must be evidenced in writing
C They need not be in writing

(1 mark)

44 In relation to the law of negligence, a finding of *volenti non fit injuria* arises from the action of which of the following?

    A   The claimant
    B   The respondent
    C   A third party
    D   An unforeseeable event

                                                                                               (2 marks)

45 In the context of the law of contract, which TWO of the following statements in relation to a letter of comfort are correct?

    (1)   It is a binding promise to pay a subsidiary company's future debts
    (2)   It is a non-binding statement of present intention to pay a subsidiary company's future debts
    (3)   It is issued by a parent company
    (4)   It is issued by a parent company's bank

    A   1 and 3
    B   2 and 3
    C   2 and 4
    D   1 and 2

                                                                                               (2 marks)

                                                                                               (70 marks)

[P.T.O.

1   Az Ltd operates a shipbuilding business which specialises in constructing and modifying ships to order. In 2011, Az Ltd entered into an agreement with Bob to completely rebuild a ship to Bob's specification for a total contract price of £7 million. However, after completion, Bob informed Az Ltd that, due to the downturn in the world economy, he no longer needed the ship. Az Ltd had already expended £5 million on altering the ship, and immediately started an action against Bob for breach of contract.

However, in the week before the case was to be decided in the court, Az Ltd sold the ship for the same amount of money which they would have received from Bob.

Required:

(a)   **State the purposes of awarding damages for breach of contract.**   (2 marks)

(b)   **State the duty to mitigate losses.**   (2 marks)

(c)   **State the level of damages Az Ltd can claim for breach of contract.**   (2 marks)

                                                                                                        (6 marks)

2   Clare, Dan and Eve formed a partnership 10 years ago, although Clare was a sleeping partner and never had anything to do with running the business. Last year Dan retired from the partnership. Eve has subsequently entered into two large contracts. The first one was with a longstanding customer, Greg, who had dealt with the partnership for some five years. The second contract was with a new customer, Hugh. Both believed that Dan was still a partner in the business. Both contracts have gone badly wrong, leaving the partnership owing £50,000 to both Greg and Hugh. Unfortunately the business assets will only cover the first £50,000 of the debt.

Required:

(a)   **State the liability of Clare as a sleeping partner.**   (2 marks)

(b)   **Identify the liabilities of Dan as a retiring partner.**   (2 marks)

(c)   **State from whom Greg can claim the outstanding debt.**   (2 marks)

                                                                                                        (6 marks)

3 Jon, who is 65 years of age, has just retired from his employment with a pension and a lump sum payment of £100,000. He is keen to invest his money but has absolutely no knowledge of business or investment. He does not wish to take any great risk with his investment but he would like to have a steady flow of income from it.

He has been advised that he can invest in the following range of securities:

(1) Preference shares
(2) Ordinary shares
(3) Debentures secured by a fixed charge
(4) Debentures secured by a floating charge.

Required:

In relation to the above investment forms:

(a) Identify which is the most secure.   (2 marks)

(b) State which may have a cumulative right to dividends.   (2 marks)

(c) State which NORMALLY participates in surplus capital.   (2 marks)

                                                                                              (6 marks)

4 In 2008 Ger was disqualified from acting as a company director for a period of 10 years under the Company Directors Disqualification Act 1986 for engaging in fraudulent trading.

However, he decided to continue to pursue his fraudulent business and, in order to avoid the consequences of the disqualification order, he arranged for his accountant Kim to run the business on his instructions. Although Kim took no shares in the company, and was never officially appointed as a director, he nonetheless assumed the title of managing director.

Required:

(a) Identify which of the following categories of directors apply to Ger and Kim:

   (i)   *De facto*
   (ii) *De jure*
   (iii) **Non-executive**
   (iv) **Shadow.**   (4 marks)

(b) State the working relationship and duties of non-executive directors.   (2 marks)

                                                                                              (6 marks)

5 Fran and Gram registered a private limited company, Ire Ltd, in January 2009, with each of them becoming a director of the company.

Although the company did manage to make a small profit in its first year of trading, it was never a great success and in its second year of trading it made a loss of £10,000.

At that time Fran said he thought the company should cease trading and be wound up. Gram, however, was insistent that the company would be profitable in the long term so they agreed to carry on the business, with Fran taking less of a part in the day-to-day management of the company, although retaining his position as a company director.

In the course of the next three years Gram falsified Ire Ltd's accounts to disguise the fact that the company had continued to suffer losses, until it became obvious that he could no longer hide the company's debts and that it would have to go into insolvent liquidation, with debts of £100,000.

Required:

(a) **State whether criminal or civil action, or both, can be taken in relation to fraudulent trading and wrongful trading.** (2 marks)

(b) **Explain whether Fran or Gram will be liable for either of the following:**

    (i) **Fraudulent trading under s.213 Insolvency Act 1986;**
    (ii) **Wrongful trading under s.214 Insolvency Act 1986.** (4 marks)

(6 marks)

End of Question Paper

Answers

Section A

1   A
2   B
3   B
4   A
5   C
6   B
7   B
8   A
9   B
10 A
11 B
12 B
13 A
14 B
15 B
16 C
17 B
18 B
19 C
20 A
21 D
22 A
23 B
24 D
25 B
26 D
27 B
28 A
29 D
30 C
31 C
32 C
33 B
34 C
35 B
36 C
37 D
38 A
39 C
40 B
41 B
42 C
43 C
44 A
45 B

Section B

1   **(a)**   Damages in contract are intended to compensate an injured party for any financial loss sustained as a consequence of another
             party's breach. The object is not to punish the party in breach, so the amount of damages awarded can never be greater than
             the actual loss suffered. The usual aim of the award of damages is to put the injured party in the same position they would
             have been in had the contract been properly performed (expectation loss).

    (b)   The duty to mitigate losses ensures that the injured party is under a duty to take all reasonable steps to minimise their loss.
             As a result, the seller of goods, which are not accepted, has not only to try to sell the goods to someone else but is also
             required to get as good a price as they can when they sell them (*Payzu* v *Saunders* (1919)). If goods are not delivered under
             a contract, the buyer is entitled to go into the market and buy similar goods, paying the market price prevailing at the time.
             They can then claim the difference in price between what they paid and the original contract price as damages.

(c) Applying the foregoing to the contract between Az Ltd and Bob, it can be seen that Az Ltd managed to recoup all of the costs and potential profit it would have made on the contract with Bob, so is not in a position to claim any further damages from Bob.

2 **(a)** Her status as a sleeping partner gives Clare no additional protection from the unlimited liability which applies to all ordinary partners in an ordinary partnership. It simply means she has left her personal wealth open to clams over which she has no practical control through her own inaction.

(b) He remains liable to *existing* customers until those customers are informed that he has left the partnership.

He also remains liable to *new* customers who knew he was a member of the partnership, unless he has made public his withdrawal.

(c) Greg can claim from all three parties: Clare, Dan and Eve.

3 **(a)** As loans, debentures are more secure than shares. Debentures secured by fixed charges are more secure than those secured by floating charges. Consequently, debentures secured by fixed charges are the most secure form of investment of those listed. They do, however, receive the least in terms of return.

(b) Of the four investment forms only shares receive dividends, as debentures receive interest due to the fact that they are forms of loan. Of the share forms only the preference share can carry a right to a cumulative dividend, as ordinary shares only get a return on the profits generated by the company in any particular year.

(c) Only shares have any claim against surplus capital, as debentures are only secured against the amount loaned.

Of the two types of shares, preference shares MAY have rights to enjoy access to surplus capital but ONLY ordinary shares have such facility as a right.

4 **(a)** Ger acts behind the scenes and is clearly operating as a shadow director. Kim has not been appointed as such but acts as a director, which makes him a *de facto* director.

(b) As with all directors, non-executives owe fiduciary duties (now stated in statute) to their company. They are also subject to all legal regulation applying to ordinary directors. They may attend company meetings and have full voting rights.

5 **(a)** Criminal liability is only applicable to fraudulent trading under the Companies Act 2006. However, civil action is open under ss.213 and 214 Insolvency Act 1986 in relation to both fraudulent and wrongful trading.

(b) As a consequence of his falsification of the accounts, Gram is potentially liable under s.213 Insolvency Act 1986 fraudulent trading provisions.

Fran, on the other hand, may not have been liable for fraud but is certainly liable for wrongful trading for not taking the appropriate action to prevent the subsequent losses sustained by the company.

Section A

1–45   One or two marks per question; total marks 70

Section B

1   **(a)**   1 mark for each relevant point made relating to damages up to the maximum 2 marks.

    (b)   1 mark for each relevant point made relating to the duty to mitigate losses, up to the maximum 2 marks.

    (c)   1 mark for correct application and 1 mark for explanation.

2   **(a)**   1 mark for each relevant point made relating to the potential liability of Clare as a sleeping partner, up to the maximum 2 marks.

    (b)   1 mark for each relevant point made relating to the potential liability of Dan as a retired partner, up to the maximum 2 marks.

    (c)   Full 2 marks only to be given to a fully correct answer.

        Partial answers to be limited to 1 mark.

3   **(a)**   1 mark for correct statement and 1 mark for explanation.

    (b)   1 mark for correct statement and 1 mark for explanation of cumulative rights.

    (c)   1 mark for correct statement and 1 mark for explanation of surplus capital.

4   **(a)**   3–4 marks for a complete explanation of the different types of director and a correct application to Ger and Kim.

        1–2 marks for some understanding but lacking either application or explanation.

        0 marks for no understanding of the substance of the question.

    (b)   1 mark for each relevant point made relating to the role/function of non-executive directors, up to the maximum 2 marks.

5   **(a)**   A full answer distinguishing between fraudulent and wrongful trading is required for both marks to be given.

        1 mark for any relevant point made relating to either action.

    (b)   4 marks for a full answer clearly distinguishing the two types of activity and correctly applying them.

        1 mark each for correctly stating how each provision will be applied to the parties.

        1 mark for any relevant point made relating to either party's action.